MAKE A POEM CRY

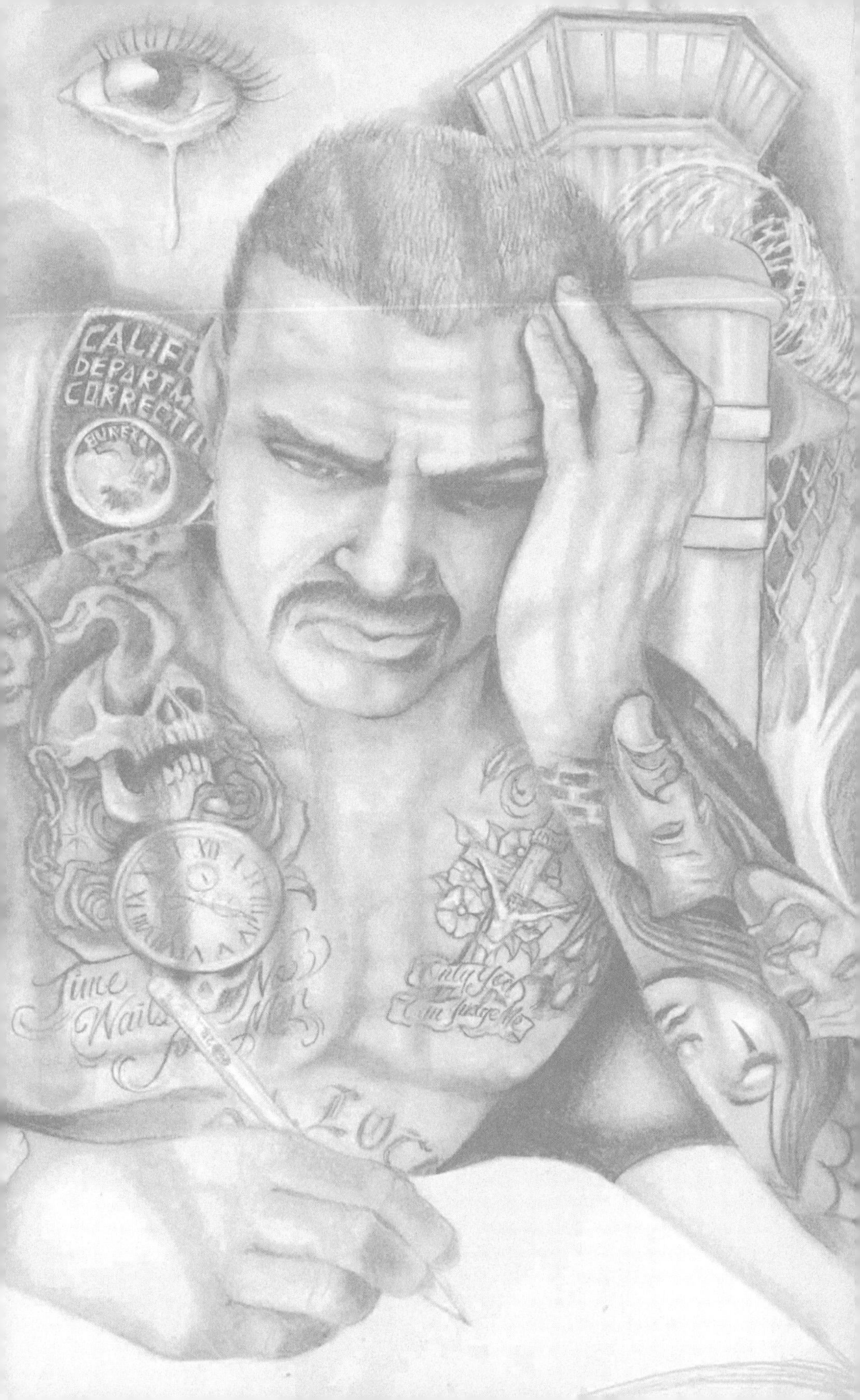
CALIF
DEPARTM
CORRECTI
Time
Waits
No
Man
Only You
Can Judge Me

MAKE A POEM CRY

CREATIVE WRITING FROM CALIFORNIA'S LANCASTER PRISON

EDITED BY
Kenneth E. Hartman
and
Luis J. Rodriguez

ISBN: 978-1-882688-58-6

Book Design: Jane Brunette
Cover art: "The Blank Page" by Manuel Cardenas

Published Tía Chucha Press, a project of Tía Chucha's Centro Cultural, Inc.
PO Box 328, San Fernando, CA 91341.
www.tiachucha.org

Distributed by: Northwestern University Press
Chicago Distribution Center 11030 South Langley Avenue Chicago IL 60628

Tía Chucha's Centro Cultural & Bookstore is a 501 (c) (3) nonprofit corporation funded in part over the years by the Arts for Justice Fund, National Endowment for the Arts, California Arts Council, Los Angeles County Arts Commission, Los Angeles Department of Cultural Affairs, The California Community Foundation, the Annenberg Foundation, the Weingart Foundation, the Lia Fund, National Association of Latino Arts and Culture, Ford Foundation, MetLife, Southwest Airlines, the Andy Warhol Foundation for the Visual Arts, the Thrill Hill Foundation, the Middleton Foundation, Center for Cultural Innovation, John Irvine Foundation, Not Just Us Foundation, the Attias Family Foundation, and the Guacamole Fund, Arts for Justice Fund, among others. Donations have also come from Bruce Springsteen, John Densmore of The Doors, Jackson Browne, Lou Adler, Richard Foos, Gary Stewart, Charles Wright, Adrienne Rich, Tom Hayden, Dave Marsh, Jack Kornfield, Jesus Trevino, David Sandoval, Gary Soto, Denise Chávez and John Randall of the Border Book Festival, Luis & Trini Rodríguez, and more.

CONTENTS

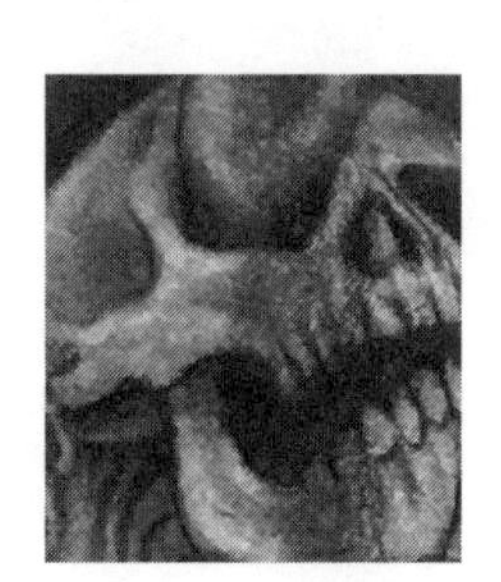

PREFACE

KENNETH E. HARTMAN

Why Words Matter

B*UT words will never hurt me*, is how one 19th century childhood rhyme went, the last phrase after the broken bones from the sticks and stones had been invoked to minimize the impact of mere words. Having lived a life rooted in both words and broken bones, I know how inaccurate that turns out to be in real life. Words not only can hurt; they can move mountains and bring people and empires to their knees. And they can heal, provide comfort, inspire, uplift. Words are powerful things.

There are few places left where putting pen to paper remains the dominant mode of formal communication, but so it is inside the jails and prisons of this country. Whether it's sad letters to family members, or desperate pleas to heedless courts and government functionaries, or long, passionate missives to lovers on the other side of the fences, the average man or woman in prison talks to the rest of the world through words written on paper.

The long history of writing from inside in the United States is filled with great writers, from Henry David Thoreau's *Civil Disobedience and Other Writings*, to O. Henry's *Short Stories*, to Dr. Martin Luther King, Jr.'s *Letter from a Birmingham Jail*, among many others. This imprisoned lineage can, in fact, be traced back through the centuries all over the world, to include Oscar

Wilde, Mohandas K. Gandhi, and Alexander Solzhenitsyn, among still many others, all the way back to St. Paul the Apostle in his Prison Epistles: *Ephesians*, *Philippians*, *Colossians*, and *Philemon*. Being a writer in prison is to be part of a long chain of other writers who used their pens to push back against the obscurity and horror, the insignificance and futility of imprisonment.

In my own life, as a writer working from inside of prison, I saw my role as a chronicler of what was happening around me and what that did to me, to my heart and soul. Through the detailing of what the experience of imprisonment did to me, I was able to connect to those around me in the same circumstances and, through that act of empathy, I was able to build the vocabulary to empathize with the experiences of other humans in other circumstances. Through the art of writing I was able to rehumanize myself, back to who I always was, back to the person I ought to have been all along. Through the practice of deeply thinking about what I wanted to say, putting that onto paper, and then reconsidering it, reworking it, sharing it with others, through all of that process that is writing, I became a full human being.

At the most elemental level, all of this is about words. Those remarkable atoms of the craft, the nuts and bolts of what we writers do, and what we strive to fill the blank spaces with on the sheets of paper that will hold our thoughts and dreams and prayers. Words that can describe with precision the depth of a feeling, the intensity of loss, or how much it hurts to be inside of a prison cell when your mother passes on to whatever awaits us all. Somehow, these few words we have, numbering only in the thousands, can encompass the entire universe and describe the most amorphous of things in an infinite variety of ways. They can describe the sibilance of a softly uttered sigh passing between the parted lips of a lover; they can describe what the soundless breaking of a heart feels like as your world disintegrates. Words are powerful things, indeed.

What every writer working from inside of prison would want, I believe, is to translate their experiences inside into a language that those who have never been inside can understand. They would want the reader to be able to hear the crashing metal doors and jarring alarms, smell the rank odors of fear and rage, see trapped horizons shrunken down inside of a concrete box, and feel the layers of regret and desperation that colors their lives every single day. This is what motivates the impulse of the writer, to explain what is happening around them and within them, to create chains of words that hold experiences onto pages. The prison experience is no less worthy or interesting than any other experience, rather, it is all the more compelling for its intensity and depth.

In the more than twenty-one years I served in California's Lancaster Prison, I wrote furiously and passionately in my quest to free my mind from the shackles on my body. I never thought I would be on the outside. Nevertheless, here I am in the less confined world on this side of the prison fences. It has been both a profound privilege and a serious responsibility to help mold this collection of writings from my brothers who are still in there for readers out here. You will find sadness and joy, pain and release, love and rage in between the covers of this book. In other words, you will find the human condition, delimited by high, electrified fences and quite compressed, but the human condition all the more.

There is another old proverb of uncertain origin, that seems especially apt here: *There but for the grace of God, go I.* When you read these poems, stories, and essays, recall that admonition that is also a call for compassion.

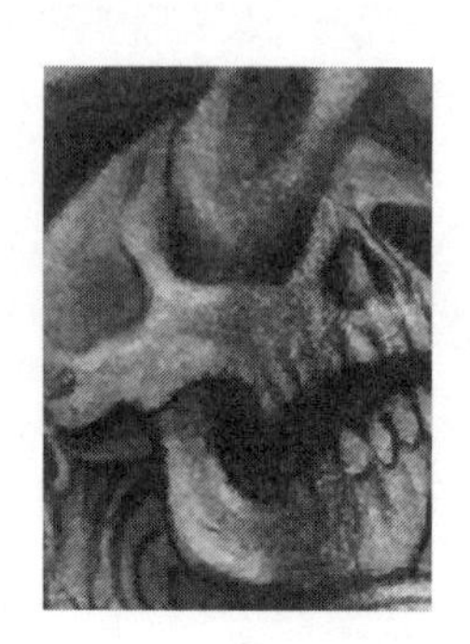

INTRODUCTION

LUIS J. RODRÍGUEZ

The Tip of the Iceberg

I can't see 'em coming from my eye,
so I had to make this poem cry.
–JIMMY MCMILLAN,
AN INCARCERATED POET IN
CALIFORNIA'S PRISON SYSTEM.

YOU CAN chain the body, the face, the eyes, the way hands move coarsely over cement or deftly on tattooed skin with needle. You can cage the withered membrane, the withered dream, the way razor wire, shouts, yells, and batons can wither spirit.

But how can you imprison a poem? How can a melody be locked up, locked down? Yes, even caged birds sing, even grass sprouts through asphalt, even a flower blooms in a desert. And the gardens of trauma we call the incarcerated can also spring with the vitality of a deep thought, an emotion buried beneath the facades deep as rage, deep as grief, the grief beneath all rages.

The blood of such poems, songs, emotions, thoughts, dances, are what flow in all art, stages, films, books. The keys to liberation are in the heart, in the mind, behind the cranial sky. The imagination is boundless, the inexhaustible in any imprisoned system.

If only the contrived freedoms society professes can flow from such water! The path to peace is art, arrows puncturing the phantoms that haunt ghettos, barrios, trailer parks, reservations, migrant camps, homeless enclaves, forcing poverty of things into poverty of spirit.

Drugs, belief-systems, illusions of a world magnitude, are not as powerful or lasting as the solidity of dreams. So, when you can't see a tear drop from an eye, let a poem cry, the paper bleed, an image or chant exorcise the demons of despair.

A bit of history: I've been teaching creative writing as well as doing poetry readings, talks, and healing circles in prisons, juvenile lockups, and jails for forty years. I began in the California Institution for Men in Chino, CA in the fall of 1980, at the invitation of Manual "Manazar" Gamboa. Manazar took me under his wing as he facilitated writing workshops in the barrios of Highland Park, Echo Park, East Los Angeles, as well as juvenile hall and prison. I met Manazar two years before during writing workshops of the Los Angeles Latino Writers Association (LALWA). In LALWA we organized a Chicano poetry reading series, bringing such notables of the time as Lorna Dee Cervantez, Gary Soto, and Jose Montoya, and facilitating the Barrio Writers Workshops. We also produced the literary arts magazine *ChismeArte* (Gossip Art) with a collective of artists and writers including Helena María Viramontes, Jesús Mena, Victor M. Valle, Barbara Carrasco, Naomi Quiñonez, and Guillermo Bejarano. Manazar and I established a public radio program for KPFK-FM called "Corazon de Aztlan" (Heart of Aztlan). And in the early 80s we helped found one of the first art gallery/performance spaces in Echo Park called Galeria Ocaso (Sunset Gallery) on East Sunset Boulevard.

Now, across four decades, I've talked to incarcerated men, women, and youth at Los Angeles County's Eastlake, Nidorf, and Los Padrinos juvenile halls; Youth Authority Prisons such as Nelles, Chino's Youth Training School, and in Ventura County (before most of these were closed down); L.A. County probation youth camps of Gonzalez, Kirkpatrick, Miller, and Challengers; youth lockups or jails in San Jose, Oakland, San Francisco, San Mateo, San Diego, Santa Ana, among others; and adult prisons of San Quentin, Folsom, Soledad, Lancaster, and California Institution for Women in Chino. I've also done the same in youth and adult facilities in Nevada, Washington, Oregon, Arizona, New Mexico, Texas, Ohio, Illinois, Michigan, Wisconsin, Nebraska, Pennsylvania, Connecticut, New Jersey, Delaware, North Carolina, Virginia, and Louisiana.

Due to my reputation in this field, I've also visited ten prisons and a juvenile detention center in El Salvador across 27 years of reporting on and working with *maras* (street gangs). I've entered two prisons in Guatemala with members of Homeboy Industries of Los Angeles. And with the help of the US Consulate's Cultural Attaché program, I talked and read poetry in a prison in Chihuahua, Mexico and a juvenile hall in Ciudad Juarez as well as five prisons/youth institutions in Argentina. On another occasion I spent three days at Her Majesty's Young Offender Institution in southern England—and once oversaw a writing session with juvenile offenders in Rome, Italy.

From 2007-2008, California's Arts in Corrections program invited me to teach creative writing at California State Prison-Los Angeles County (also known as Lancaster State Prison) in the only Honor Yard at the time of the vast 34-prison state system. After a long hiatus, I returned in the fall of 2016 to work for the Alliance for California Traditional Arts (ACTA) in facilitating creative writing classes in two high security yards at the same institution. The writings in this anthology come from the early sessions at Lancaster from 2016 to 2018.

My thanks to the California Department of Corrections and Rehabilitation for opening the door to this opportunity. To Amy Kitchener, Executive Director of the Alliance for California Traditional Arts, and her staff—ACTA also brings in dancers, weavers, storytellers, musicians, and artists to various prisons and other institutions throughout the state. Much respect to the wonderful team, headed by Rebecca Gomez, of Tia Chucha's Centro Cultural's Trauma to Transformation Program, which teaches arts, writing, and theater in prisons—male and female—as well as juvenile halls, parolee housing, probation schools, and to families of the incarcerated. Trauma to Transformation exist with the generous support of the Arts for Justice Fund, California Arts Council, and National Endowment for the Arts.

And thanks to Jessica Wilson Cardenas, Tia Chucha Press' Coordinator, and my youngest son Luis "Chito" Rodriguez for helping input this material.

For those who may not know, my wife Trini and I helped create Tia Chucha's Centro Cultural & Bookstore in 2001, a culmination of a dream I've had since first working with Manazar in the late 1970s. This center is also the present home of Tia Chucha Press, which I began in Chicago over 30 years ago, and publisher of this anthology.

And, finally, my immense gratitude to those writers who contributed to this book, including those who submitted work, but unfortunately, could not be included due to space and other factors. This anthology contains a sampling—the tip of the iceberg—of the many voices, stories, poems, and expressions that have yet to be tapped from among some of the most silenced members of our communities. This is a powerful showcase of what's possible when the arts—painting, music, writing, dance, and theater—are used as redemptive tools for renewing, transforming, and putting back together formerly fractured and lost lives.

In the end, this shows they are creative beings in process, works of art. The ultimate masterpiece is them.

GILBERT BAO

Tamales | A Family Tradition

Lessons in my Roots...

Ever since I can remember, my Nana (Grandma) cooked tamales during Christmas and New Year holidays. The distinct aroma of boiling *colorado chiles*, *carne*, and the fresh-made *masa* (maiz) is synonymous to the holiday season as it is to any family gathering at Nana's house.

Nana knew all the special places to get the ingredients to make tamales. I would go with her to the *Maravilla Carniceria* (a local meat market) and carry the large bowls for the masa, an important task for a young boy. The *carniceria* is located at the intersection of Arizona Boulevard and Avenida Cesar Chavez in East Los Angeles. It was a magical place with Chicano/Mexicano murals adorning the walls and loud Mexican *corridos* (ballads) spilling into the air. As we enter, there are colorful *piñatas* hanging from the ceiling and a good chance of Nana buying me Mexican *dulce* (candy). My favorite *dulce* is *chile paletas*—they are the equivalent to the American lollipop/sucker, but flavored with *chile*.

At home there was usually a full house of family or friends living there. Nana never said no to anyone who needed a place to live. She was the sixth of 12 siblings after her parents migrated from Central Mexico to East Los Angeles during the Mexican Revolution of 1910. She told me she learned how to make tamales from her mother—I wondered how long the tradition had been passed down from each of the generations in my family.

I do not remember Nana ever saying she was going to show me how to make tamales. The lessons were handed down to me as I grew up in her house and I helped prepare them each year. Nana's kitchen would come alive as she gathered all the special utensils stored deep in the cabinets or stashed in the washer and dryer closet because of their large sizes. The big *ollas* (pots) are used to cook tamales, menudo, *albondigas* (meatballs), and *frijoles* (beans). Then there is the large cone-shaped strainer with wooden roller to grind the *chiles* after they are boiled—that was usually my job.

As each step in the process is performed, Nana explains the importance of the flavoring, never using measuring utensils, only her memory, and giving me the latest gossip about family members, both as complaints and how proud she was of them. There is a buzz that goes around the family when they are planning out their trips from home to home, everyone knowing that when they reach Nana's they will be enjoying her delicious and famous tamales.

Cultural Connections...

For many cultures around the world, food is an important staple of bonding between family and communities. Nana often sent me to neighbors' homes with tamales to share with close friends as there were other families who shared their tamales with us. Tamales are originated from the indigenous peoples of Mexico and Central America. The origin of the word tamale derived from the word *tamalli* in the Nahuatl language. Nahuatl is the mother tongue of Mexico. It continues to be the most widely spoken indigenous language in North America despite the false claim that Spain conquered the Aztecs and they no longer exist.

I learned the origins and history of tamales during my present incarceration. In the 19 years of living in a cell, away from my family, I have made many efforts to keep alive the traditions of my upbringing. Reinventing a sense of home away from home has kept my spirits alive in a place designed to destroy them. In no way do I consider the cell my home—it is a place where I can merge creativity and my will to overcome the ever-present loneliness. Loneliness is most prevalent during the holidays; these are the times I miss my family most. I found a way to ease some of the pain creating a different way to make tamales.

Reaching Within...

One day while out on the prison yard, I stumbled across a prison-made tamale that did not match my memories of Nana's tamales. I asked a few questions about how the guy made his tamales—my mind started thinking about better ways to create my own version, closer to the way I remembered them tasting.

The first problem I realized was coming up with a way to cook them with a lot of heat. In the cell we are allowed to have hot-pots to heat water. But they are small and can only be plugged in for short amounts of time that produce very little heat. I solved the problem using a technique to cook prison "moonshine." I made a couple of stingers that can produce a lot of heat and stay plugged in for hours at a time. To make one all you need is an old plug cut off from a broken appliance (which will be the wire), disposable shaving razors, and a plastic trash bag. attaching the wire to the razor blades—positive on one side and negative on the other—and wrapping strips of plastic around the connections from the wire to the blades, you'll have the utensil capable of cooking the tamales. Trial and error solved many of the early problems. The recipe is the closest I can get to Nana's tamales considering the available ingredients.

On Christmas Eve, I prepare my tamales and cook them early in the morning of Christmas Day. I have taught many of my cellies to make tamales the same way I learned as a young boy. It takes a day and a half to make them. However, I believe the time and love that go into making them is what keeps me connected to family and culture. It also eases the loneliness in my heart as well as the guilt for the hurt and pain I have caused my family. I know if I feel it, they must feel it stronger because they are not the cause of me being here. I am.

So on Christmas Eve, I roll up my mattress and place it on the top bunk so I can use my bunk as a large table. I clean the bed and walls with disinfectant the prison passes out on the first and 15th of the month. I boil water in the hot-pot and crush the corn and nacho chips into a fine powder (this is a long process that can take a few hours to complete). Once the chips are crushed into a fine powder, I place them into a large plastic trash bang and insert boiling water until the masa forms into soft clay-like consistency. The summer sausages are chopped and mixed with the pouch of meat and beans so that the diced jalapeños can be placed on top.

The small trash bags are cut into 10-inch squares and placed on the bed, ten at a time. After the ball of masa is flattened onto each square—and the meat, beans, and jalapeños are rolled into the tamales—I place them on a plastic bag on the cement floor. The floor is very cold and acts as a refrigerator overnight. I noticed over the years that allowing them to sit on the cold floor overnight hardened the masa and enhanced the flavors. It takes a full day to prepare the tamales and clean up. But the cell smells almost like home. There have been many times a Correctional Officer will open the doors because of the smell and want to see what I'm doing. They are always amazed of the ingenuity when I answer their questions about the recipe.

On Christmas Day, I wake up at about 5 AM and start the cooking process. I fill up a 35 quart plastic container and submerge the stingers in the water before I plug them in. This is important or you'll blow out the power on the whole tier and have a bunch of angry neighbors who are usually cooking their own holiday meal. I put the tamales in small plastic trash bags and place them in the water for about three to four hours until the masa changes to a dark beige, and the plastic separates from the tamales with air. After they are done, I place them flat on the metal bed to cool down for 15 to 20 minutes. Then they are ready to eat.

Tamales have been around for hundreds of years, possibly thousands. They are made in the jungles, deserts, cities, towns, and now in prisons. So please stop teaching (misleading) my people to believe they were totally conquered Spain. Look at our foods, language, and customs and you'll find we are still here.

Every year Nana and my mom want to know how the tamales came out. I think it helps them to know I am not sitting in a cold cell and stressing during the holidays. Instead, I am doing my best with what I have—and not allowing the poor decisions of my past deprive me of the love that was placed in my heart by my Nana.

TAMALES

Ingredients:

Tortilla chips - (16 oz) Hometown Nacho Cheese flavor	$2.15
Corn chips - (12 oz)	$1.60
Spicy Refried Pinto Beans - (12 oz)	$1.60
American Premium Beef Summer Sausage - (4.5 oz)	$2.00
Chata-Chilorio Meat Beef/Pork - (8 oz) pouch	$4.70
Hometown Sliced Jalapeño Peppers - (12 oz)	$1.30
Velveeta Spread Cheese - (8 oz)	$3.20

Utensils:

Item	Price
Hot Pot - West Bend clear hot-pot	$22.95
Large plastic bag	
Small plastic bag	
Stinger (contraband)	
Plastic container - 28 quart or larger	$9.90
Cereal bowl - 6 to 7-inch diameter	$1.50
Razor blade (extracted from disposable shaving razor)	

Stinger Utensils:

6 razor blades (removed from disposable shaving razor)
Wire cord with plug (cut off of an appliance)
Plastic strips (cut from plastic bag)
Strip of plastic (cut from disposable shaving razor)

Stinger Directions:

Remove razor blades from disposable shaving razor
Stack three razor blades and attach a positive wire
Stack the other three razors and attach negative wire
Divide the two stacks of razors with a piece of plastic from disposable azor handle so the two stacks do not touch.
Wrap plastic strips around wire connections to razors

Cooking Directions:

Roll up mattress, put it on the top bunk, and disinfect the bed with Cell Block 40.
Crush chips into a fine powder, and place in a large plastic trash bag (Porter gets bags from Correctional Officer).
Boil beef sausage and pouch meat in Hot Pot.
Cut small bags into 10-inch squares with razor blade.
Cut Velveeta Cheese into 12 slices.

Place boiling water into crushed chips and mix until it forms into a consistent masa.

Sprinkle the metal bed with water and place 10 of the cut bags onto the wet surface.

Form masa into the size of a baseball and flatten on to each plastic bag, inch thickness.

Place cereal bowl over flattened masa (upside down) and press to make perfect circle. Remove excess masa.

Place a handful of meat with beans in the center and insert a piece of cheese.

Fold tamale in half and apply small amount of pressure at the seam.

Fold excess bag at top and roll over to complete tamale.

Place tamales in small bag, tie (air tight), and place into plastic container for boiling.

Submerge tamales into water and boil approximately three to four hours.

You will know when they are done when the masa changes to dark beige and the plastic wrap separates.

Pull tamales out of bag and let cool down 15 to 20 minutes before eating. This is the time the masa hardens.

D. BARRY

Irezumi | Japanese-style tattooing

A world that is taboo and seen, but unheard of
A society within itself were bonds are formed and codes are followed
A master craftsman sits in his element
A tray laid out with tools of the trade
Plastic caps with liquid splash
Hand-crafted machines sit ready and willing
Century old images being used and transformed into
    21st-century motifs
Each one a different meaning for the brave soul
Who is willing to defy the social norm
A thousand practices turn into a million masterpieces
Oh, the sweet joy of this pain I feel
Pleasure and pain becoming ecstasy
Technique meets free flow
A gushing waterfall of ideas and wonder
The smooth rhythm of needles meeting flesh
Fierce dragons and roaring tigers
Soaring falcons and flying phoenixes
Upstream kois and downward turtles
Bringing luck, warding off evil
Paying homage to ancestors and respecting the gods
A secret world where messages are hidden
and hidden messages broadcasted like a silent alarm
Oh, the sweet feeling of needles meeting flesh
This wonderful world of *irezumi*

D. BARRY

When Destiny meets Fate

SITTING IN A concrete box that echoes past screams and reading the nicks that hold the history of this concrete box. Waiting and waiting for the hours to pass and the hands to tick by, yearning to hear the scrape of boots and the clinging of keys in the far distance. Understanding the cog and mechanics of the concrete monster where souls get lost and found. So bored you start counting the bricks in the wall and you start thinking about the past, the good, the bad, and the ugly. Old resentments coming boiling to the surface making you rethink the universe. Wait... you hear that? Someone calling in the distance, ears prick up like a dog. Searching for that sweet voice calling you, you answer back with a hint of joy in your voice, just happy to be connecting with the world again.

Sitting in a concrete box that echoes past screams and reading the nicks that hold the history of this concrete box. Finding the pathway to connect to others you build a service line using what you got, then a highway is built and others who seek the same find the highway of information. Information is given to you and it's absorbed as quickly as a dying man in the desert, eager for that wonderful knowledge that quenches our thirst. Becoming happier and healthier as we continue to drink from this fountain. Man's creations sprawled across the pages of wonder and awe, the simple idea of something beautiful being created, understanding the tricks and techniques incorporated to fool the eye. Masterpieces begetting from manifestations of many minds, the excitement of learning something new and testing out theories

Newfound knowledge creates a new world to live in, many wonders and many struggles. A new patch unfolds where nothing was ever thought of, mind and soul being sent through the pages of creations and time immemorial. Seeking happiness where none other can bring, finding destiny and making it fate. Finally, finding the keys to the locked door and stepping through, escaping this concrete box where so many yearn to hear the scrape of the boot and clinging of keys. Forever following the new path and never looking back. Happy that mind and soul are finally one.

IRA BENJAMIN

Dangerous

OH, HOW THIS savagery caught on, the havoc incubated in war zones. Told we were accidents, wonder if that's why our actions practice a despondent form of being desperate. Oh, what this desperation feeds, living reckless, just so I can have rhymes to go along with those beats, just so I can have some bread go along with this meat. Just so I can justify why I got blood blistering my feet. We products of this concrete, being told to be meek so we can inherit what it is we can't see. Got us flipping over cop cars, setting fires in these streets cause the only future written in our stars got us walking a penitentiary yard and turning into beasts. How long do we have to exclaim? Sending projectile objects, taking aim, displacing our targets, projecting our pain. Wonder if this is why we're mistaken as being heartless, portraying this story of Cain, written off as a margin, being factionless, us in the search of our names. How come our cries seem to not matter, unless they're accompanied machine gun chatter? How come we're not categorized as victims of war crimes? Illustrated the "random" blood splatter. Memorialized with candle visuals, reminding us we don't count as individuals. The only emotion left to identify with creates our chaos, our anger rages in us, hostile, cuz we're proved and labeled *dangerous*!!!

IRA BENJAMIN

Blinded

WHO ARE you? Like, what's your meaning? Like, if you could press rewind and see it all from the beginning. What would your definition be? Am I heartless because I don't feel tears at the sight of tragedy? Am I a projected image of all that has affected me? Am I a product of the slums, infested with drugs which numb us to become these common irregularities? Under the makeup that perfects the blemishes, the women who raise boys into men, teach us to mask our indecencies. So how do I know my nature? What's a viable option? When your mother in marinated in toxins and she's been teaching you the same since you were in her arms, rocking. Now I'm searching for absolution, hopefully I'll find recognition in this penance before the conclusion. Cause I been suppressing my resentment, letting it fester till it bulges up, ill-content, because all my nourishment has been poisonous. Just realizing my tolerance has a double edge and I been teetering, toes creeping over a ledge, waiting for the blade that's been pressing down on my neck. When do you recognize that every act you justified is another potential wreck? Moments lost, substituted out your life, to only be replaced all that was behind the lie. That lie of the truth, not being what you seen, like it ain't true. It ain't true your mother was a prostitute, so now you see these girls as another dime you'll lose. Say it ain't true and every step taken hasn't been influenced to move, like your finger ain't on that trigger just to get approved and you ain't been told not to pull that gun unless it's going to be used. Who we trying to fool? Cause I can't tell me this ain't true. I feel my sins, OCD kicking in. And I'm unclean, afflicted, because I was caught in between what was intended and what wasn't seen. Call it being blinded.

IRA BENJAMIN

Social Commentary

Wait! Hands up. Don't shoot, I got something to lose. I'm not going to run because of that gun. It ain't a taser, and my life I'm not ready to wager on whether or not your temperament is racist. I'm cool. I don't want to be one of those cases, sensationalizing social media until it's only brought up as you scroll Wikipedia. Officer, I got something to live for–and I don't have nothing to do with filling your bank statement. Or filling these newscasts with hot-button topics that cause riots with looting and burning stores. Look, I'm showing you my back–you can relax. And take your itchy finger off that trigger. Just calm down for a minute and try to consider. I'm the same age as your son will be in just a few more years. I got a mother too. I'd like to one day have a career. If you took the time to look, you'd see I'm no crook. I'm a frightened boy, just as afraid as you are. But you're the one employed. To serve and protect, yet, you out here wearing a vest, which is illegal for me to wear over my chest. You're the one aiming a firearm with the intent to do harm. I'm shaking because you're thinking I'm black, suspicious, enough to make your head scream. I'm just trying to live, sir, so tell me–where is this headed? What do I got to give, since my word don't mean shit? What I got to do to show you that I'm innocent and misrepresented what you were previously presented. I ain't them just cause my pants sag, I walk with swag, and got a few tattoos. I'm a kid with potential, working to attain credentials. This traffic stop, Mr. Cop, is on every camera on this block–don't you know, we in a residential?

SAMUAL NATHANIEL BROWN

My Six Strings

Assignment: See yourself as a guitar with six strings. The guitar has gotten out of tune as a result of playing it over the course of your life. What are your six strings that need tuning? How does life look and feel when they are out of tune? How does life look and feel when they are in tune? How do you tune them?

MY SIX strings are my spiritual faculty, my mental faculty, my physical faculty, my emotional faculty, learning, and health.

Those are the six strings of this guitar called me.

When they are not out of tune, life looks one-dimensional and feels like torture. My spirit is chief amongst all strings and when it is out of tune, I can't sing a song of praise to my Creator, nor spiritually intuit the words required to sing a song of encouragement to others during their time of need. My mental is the second string because it allows me to assist all that is before me and move in accordance with my divine purpose. When it is not properly tuned, it means I am not able to think clearly and make good decisions that reflect my higher nature.

My third string is my physical body. This string is key to me composing songs that I can dance to and physically display my spiritual and mental consciousness. When it is out of tune I am not as efficient and productive as I can be. The fourth string on my guitar is my emotional faculty. This is a very important string that is critical to the way in which I see myself and perceive the world around me. When it is out of tune, I sing angry songs of heartache and self-destruction.

The fifth string is my ability to learn. When it is out of tune it means I am not learning. If I am not learning that I am not able to sing antiquated songs and can neither understand, nor sing, songs that are capable of transcending time and space. My six and final string is my ability to help others. When this string is out of tune, I cannot play a chord in the song of human evolution.

How to Tune Them:

In order to tune my spiritual string, I humble myself and get back to my goal of keeping my ego subdued and removed from the equation. Over the course of my life, I have learned my ego is what knocks this string out of tune. I may be faced with all manners of opposition, but in the end none of that external opposition has the ability to break my spirit or decrease its potency. My ego prevents me from submitting to God and in doing so I weaken my life force. That is to say I weaken my spirit and reduce my potential for making beautiful music. I tune this string meditating, praying, communion, summoning, and submitting to the God inside of me.

To tune my mental string, I relax and take on the same activities as I do when I need to tune my spiritual string. Over the years I have learned that sometimes I can tune this string first focusing on the string directly above it or immediately after it. There have been times when I did not know what to do in order to tune my mental string, therefore I would go exercise or clean up—physical string—and it would give me a way in and an idea of what to do next. Other times, I would meditate and pray—spiritual string—which would give me a way into my mental and show me what to do next. To tune my physical, I clean and exercise. If this isn't something I can dive directly into, then I begin with the strings above it, the mental and spiritual strings.
After I tune them, I am then able to go work out, stretch, practice yoga, breathing activities, write, or just walk and think. Whatever I feel I need to do in order to ease back into being tuned.

In order to tune my emotional string, I tune the three strings directly above it. It is easier to be in tuned emotionally when I feel I am functioning optimally spiritually, mentally, and physically. I can begin writing a song using the first three strings and listen to the way the emotional string sounds when it is struck, and immediately recognize that it is out of tune. Thus, I will consciously tune it until it is in harmony with the others. I do this engaging in intra-personal dialogue and effectively communicating how I am feeling to others I trust. Finally, I also write essays, poems, journals, and songs that express how I feel.

I tune my learning string humbling myself and bringing remembrance for all that I know—I actually know nothing. Thus, I make myself available to learn more. I read, watch educational presentations, engage people who are more knowledgeable than I am, and set educational goals for myself. I tune my helping string doing just that—helping others. I help others doing anything and everything I imagine would help better their day in a positive way. Once upon a time, I was the exact opposite. I used to be selfish and sought to do harm to others. Therefore, to tune this string I simply do the opposite of what I used to do. I lend a listening ear. I give what I can, insight if I have it. I share my personal experiences. I don't judge and I keep my interactions honest and respectful. That is how I tune my helping string.

Conclusion:

When all of my strings are tuned, I live a productive and loving life. It is purpose-filled; my thoughts and actions are efficient.

SAMUAL NATHANIEL BROWN

Yum | God-Given

Endangered life's disappointments I was faced with a decision,
a captive held captive previous choices I made that landed me
in prison.

With the potential of leading a life full of disappointment looming,
I fell into the habit of being pressured into speculating and
assuming.

I speculated my family viewed me dis-favorably as a burden;
this erroneous perception led me to feeling I needed fast money
and serving...

Drugs, fast-talk, and other criminal acts were the hallmark of a
disappointing life, wrought with jealousy, strife, and a back
well-acquainted with the top of a friendly knife.

Wake-up call, this endangerment was only as real as I made it to be,
had to reassess my perception of what "making it" meant to me.

Thus, I'm not endangered failure, on the contrary, I'm empowered.
Oppositions, troubles, tribulations, which set themselves before me,
get devoured!

SAMUAL NATHANIEL BROWN

I found, I learned | God-Given

Locked in my mind, I found the skeleton key to the outside world.
At an LL Cool J concert, I learned I could excite girls peeling off
my jacket to reveal a bare chest while saying the words, "let my
love unfurl."

In Desire Projects, I got acquainted with degradation.
In New Orleans, I learned segregation.
In a multitude of books, I learned how to erect a nation.
I realized I was in prison when I thought I was free.
I found freedom in prison–ironically.

In knowledge, I found power. In wisdom, I found love.
In understanding, I met patience, tolerance, and trust in God above...
and below, side to side, and in the last and in the first.
In surahs, verse, and testimonies, I found God in the entire universe.

In anger, I found bad decisions and pent up rage, and lack
of vocabulary taught me profanity. But in a multi-ethnic multitude
of faces, I found humanity.

SAMUAL NATHANIEL BROWN

Sagacity | God-Given

Far seeing wisdom.
That is, wisdom beyond one's years,
practical insight
capable of abating fears, preventing tears.

Tears of regret,
fears of the uncertain.
If the whole world is a stage then
birth is the opening curtain.

–Break a leg–

DARRYL BURNSIDE

No More Massacres

Dedicated to the victims of gun violence

First, this is not a method for cowards. It does resist. The nonviolent resistance is just as strongly opposed to the evil against which we protest as in the person who uses violence. This method is passive or non-aggressive in the sense that we are not physically aggressive towards our opponent. But our mind and emotions are always active, constantly seeking to persuade the opponent that he is mistaken. This method is passive physically but strongly active spiritually. It is not aggressive physically but dynamically aggressive spiritually.

–Dr. Martin Luther King, Jr.

No longer do I spread a message of violence,
not even in silence.
My old testament
was shoot anyone for whatever reason.
My community was infested with gun violence.
And I didn't take a licking;
just the sound alone created fear in my head.
Still I didn't submit.
Unfortunately, I found myself at 13
in a hospital,
a victim of gun violence,
bleeding,
shaking my head–
like dang, what's the reason?
Started holstering a gun for All Seasons.
Morals became corrupted,
trapped,
in reaction, without Law & Order,
secretly, tactically, preparing for war.
Cuz there's brutality all over the world.
See, in my ghettos, we groom to-be Killers.
Black-on-black killings.

Hearts full of madness
cuz we misguided from youth.
But ever since Congresswoman Gabrielle Gifford got shot,
and that little girl, Christina Taylor Greene,
who was with her, died,
I died a little inside.
Truly, it was then
when I realized
that my head was divided from truth.
I became teary-eyed.
My new testament begins...
Now I'm picking up the shattered pieces,
digging through the rubbish of my rearview,
face-to-face with my own demons.
please forgive me for my mishaps.
Reality check–
no more 21-gun salute,
hands up don't shoot.
I'm motivated to be a positive man.
Now can you tell me the same about you.
Please don't send the troops.
Can I get a moment of silence?
For all the victims of gun violence?
Pay attention to all the pro-gun ads across the nation,
covered with kind pleasures,
designed to take over your mind.
But I stand with Councilwoman Janice Hahn,
keeping Columbine, Sandy Hook,
Las Vegas shooting victims–
them 17 kids in Parkland,
10 in Santa Fe, Texas,
them church shootings in Charleston and Texas–
in remembrance.
Let's stand up for our little cubs.
It touched my heart
when Emma Gonzalez and Edna Chavez led the march
to Washington
to approach Congress.

They ignited the walkouts of classrooms in all 50 states
in a fight to ban assault weapons.
Look how we took it to another level,
reuniting as one,
cause the willing stopped chilling
and became willing.
So please get up
and don't give up, politicians.
Please stand up for us.
An America's Got Talent contestant, Flau 'Jae, said it best
"*Let's put down the guns.*"

DARRYL BURNSIDE

Trapped Inside a Pill

Dedicated to kids affected ADHD, ADD, and autism

TRYING TO figure out this feeling? This feeling is faulty and weakening–why can't they understand? Tell me can you understand how it feels to be caged inside a pill?

It's like I'm in a comatose state: I can hear you, but I give no reaction. It's like I'm runnin' out of time, and that's no lie. Tell me what's the problem with a child running wild? And don't ridicule us cuz we can't stay focused. See it's a difficult task concentrating in class. And if you laugh, we might just act a fool in class. Please, I ask you pay attention–hyperactivity without an ounce of impulse control, most of us are cast to the wind and labeled a problem child. And please you should never call us stupid cuz we will disrespect you–and throw some blows just to let you know. This was never our intentions, but now we're forced to take a pill. That's a contradiction. Don't shed a tear for us cuz we are not happy here. That is not to our advantage, steady telling us it's needed. So, we're confined to this pill... Here's my introduction: I wasn't wellborn cuz my father didn't raise me, too busy introducing Mama to crack. It really went down like that. Sneered at behind my back in my teenage years. They say my intelligence low, self-esteem broken, which led to feelings of inadequacy. Shame and low self-worth. I rather run like Super Sonic, the Hedgehog. See I was faster than most. I wish I could have told them that rest is for the weary. Big Mama kept me close cuz she sensed I was dreary. See in this disheartening state, let me be frank–it was hard for me to cope. I felt helpless and most times like a joke. So, tell me how could there be peace? With this Ritalin wearing down and I can finally stand on my own. I'm like "catch me if you can," like Speedy Gonzales. How can I remain in the depths of solitude, trapped inside a pill?

MATTHEW CONANT

Antidote

Poison...venom...these soldiers don't need fatigues—
they rock denim.
Urban decay, gunplay, gun spray, like...
when problems arise, they only know one way—
death!
I turn on the news... they speakin' of Zika;
I turn on the blues... I kick off my sneakas.
Recline in depression, I'm swimming in pity.
My country don't love me, but I still rep my city.
I'm caught in the paradox, in need of an antidote.

Cyber bullies with fullys—
it's all hood, it's all gully,
it's all fun and games till they pop the top off your skully—
really!
But who got the remedy?
And why does the enemy keep sending me these muthafuckin' signals?
I never gave him my frequency,
but look how frequently he aids in my delinquency.
I mean ... how did he get so in sync with me?
Google? Verizon? Can you hear me now?
I dummy down,
speak less,
to the point I don't even talk, like I'm speechless.
They don't even have a horse in my race... Preakness.
I'm wide awake... sleepless.

Medicine, medicine... I need me some medicine.
I'm locked out myself, gotta get in my head again.
I went left on Twitter, went right on IG.
Forgot my own number, I need caller ID.
Digital reality.

I don't see people, I only see profiles,
duck-face selfies—I don't see no smiles.
Snap Chat Gangstaz, Facebook Junkies
Internet celebs, real life flunkies,
perception, perception... we need new perspectives.
The bullies expelled but the web trolls accepted—
everything is backwards, watch what you say.
Gotta be pro-gay...the new American way.
So watch what you say... I mean it!
Watch what you say.
The man and woman doctrine is now considered hate.
Nothing is sacred,
everything open to interpretation—
they manipulate words to support what they're chasin'.
If I like black women...does that make me racist?
Our nation is sick...what's the antidote for hatred?

Love, love, show me some love,
show me a cure for the damage we've done.
I am not innocent, I done shed blood.
But there has to be more than bullets and guns.
If I have no gun
and I'm shot by the cops...
why is this called, "a police involved shooting?"
Others weren't involved with that shooting.
It's all word play,
confusing,
misleading,
abusing the trust of the public.
The ruling class using
media to shape opinions.
Legislation is pushed despicable minions.
Get the Pixar?
A mixture of fear and hate has arose.
Who do they ask when they take all these polls?
Listen ... who do they ask when they take all these polls?
Cause they ain't never asked anybody I know
Trump is in office... let's build a wall,

just grab the pussy... I'm appalled.
Ban Muslim countries...it reflects on us all.
I ask for some love... all I get is more law.

I'm caught in the paradox, in need of an antidote.

MATTHEW CONANT

Community | Come Unity

Don't look at the wayward youth and despise their disposition.
Do not distance yourself as if you are not connected.
Their broken dreams are the broken spokes in the hub of our community.
Do not commit to the same tribalism of gang mentalities,
disowning this generation because it's not mimetic of yours.
Do not hoard your life's experience.
Don't take to the grave with you your "know-how."
If you offer no remedy
you implicitly sponsor the symptoms of diaspora.

Don't look at the disenfranchised youth with disdain,
as if they were not born of the world you created–
be it through your activism or pacifism.
Do not function as if you hold absolutely no responsibilities for their disparagement.
The energy you exert pushing them away would be better spent pulling them close.
Embark... Embrace... Employ an act of altruism!

Don't look at the struggling youth and their social distortion,
thinking their disparities are beyond rectification–
their disparities are yours!
There is no separation.
This disunity in the community is neither indestructible nor impregnable.
Do not grow weary in this time that necessitates a show of strength...
Commitment... Determination...
Dedication and sacrifice!
We cannot abandon our youth–this is not a viable option

Look at our youth with hopeful eyes.

See them as the indispensable heirs of black humanity
in which they are.
Offer them wisdom instead of criticism.
With wisdom they will critique their own ways.
Provide them with humble and selfless examples of solidarity.
Love them equally in both their shine and shadow.

The Africans fought for survival upon their arrival in America.
Without this fight for life none of us would exist.
Don't allow the struggle to be murdered at the doorstep of your mind.
Your individual success would mean nothing in the midst
of a failed people.
We are far from failed.
Yet, we've got a-ways to travel.
We'll get there... comm-unity!

MATTHEW CONANT

My Train of Life

This story was the result of a writing prompt. We were asked to describe being on the train of life and to point out three important stops or stations in that life. We also had to describe what baggage we brought to each station–and what baggage got picked up. I was put up for adoption at birth. This is my story.

A MUFFLED VOICE echoed in my head: "All aboard!" Unsure if its declaration, but feeling the surmounting pressure, I forged my way out of the terminal of birth and proceeded through an anxious swarm of activity towards my train of life. I could feel my parents behind me, prodding me forward, aggressively pushing me away from them and on towards this train. As bad as I wanted to turn around and latch on to them, I couldn't. Neither physically nor mentally. I boarded my train without ever getting to see them drop me off at the station of life.

My train whistled, let out a plume of steam from its underbelly, and came to life. I took my seat and gazed out the window across a great expanse of railways and other trains. Mine sat low, in the heart of a gloomy valley. I looked up as the many other trains streamed across beautiful plateaus that stretched the horizon as well as the majestic mountains that dominated the other side. As my train began to gather speed, I wondered where it was going? I knew right away I wanted to see the view from the mountaintop. But all I could do at this point was look up and pray my conductor would know how to get me there. A voice through a speaker filled my cabin: "100 miles to a life fulfilled! Enjoy the ride!"

I faded off to sleep.

I awoke with my head rested against the window of my cabin. The train was rounding a bend in another low valley. Dark forests rest on both sides of the track. From this vantage point, I could barely see the lead engine. The clouds of smoke blooming from its smokestack fogged my vision. A sign shop past my window, signifying my 19th mile of life was coming up. The train began to slow at the station.

I exited the train at station 19 with caution. An overwhelming premonition of death lingered within my own being. In my hand was a gun. In my sights was a young man. I left death, pain, and sorrow at that station and picked up a murder case... and a lifetime of regret. "All aboard!" I quickly ran back to the train. In my cabin, I sunk deep into my seat. The Train of Life took me away from the murder scene and on towards a dark tunnel at the base of the biggest mountain I had ever seen. And it all went black!

My body and mind jostled around in the darkness. I could feel every bump on the track. At times the darkness was a safe haven. I could hide in my cabin where nobody could see the shame I felt had been permanently etched across my face. There were other times when the darkness scared me. I understood the consuming power of darkness. At other stations in my life I have seen people get lost in it. These were some of the loneliest times in my life. I long for those miles I spent in the sunlight. I would gladly accept the bottom track, in the valley, looking up at all the others on their plateaus, mountain sides, peaks, and bridges. I began to see the beauty of looking up. It was then I started to see some light at the end of this dark tunnel I was in.

The light burst into my cabin, stinging my eyes with its radiant glow of life! I looked out my window, naturally looking up to see those mountains and plateaus I have spent the majority of my life looking up at. There were only blue skies where the mountains should have been. I slowly brought my gaze down and realized I had made it to the mountaintop! I viewed the deep valley below me. The view was absolutely breathtaking! I felt serenity along with a deep desire for all of those trains below me to see the view from this vantage point. My train slowed as a sign past my window, reading: "Mile 44."

I got off the train at the station and was immediately swarmed family and friends. The euphoric moment enhanced the side of my beautiful wife as she pointed to the destination board. It was then I realized that, although we all have to ride the train of life, we don't have to stay on the same track. If we're smart, we'll choose our destinations wisely.

As we stood in the center of the station, with tracks shooting out in every direction, I had an epiphany. I thought of all the time I had spent on the wrong track, hitting station after station and never thinking about an alternative route. I thought about all the time I spent in those valleys looking up, about those gloomy forests alongside my train and those endless smiles in the dark tunnel. I remember coming around that bend and seeing that lead engine of my train, and how the billowing smoke made it so hard to see my future and where I was going. But as I stand here looking back, I see that the smoke always dissipates! And even though we all go through miles where it seems like everybody else's journey exists on the tracks above—the mountainside, the plateaus, those magnificent bridges above us—the truth is we all experience peaks and valleys.

As I jump on this new train with its new destination, I just thank the conductor for getting me through. "All aboard! 100 miles to a fulfilled life!"

JERIMICHAEL COOLEY

This One Night

Once upon a time one Christmas Eve, a prayer was being heard
the angel of dreams.
This prayer from a father who made a mistake, never a believer,
he was no saint.
The angel took this message straight to the throne; he spoke to God
in an excited tone.
This prayer is from one who should be damned, for in his life
he slayed a man.
Please, oh, please allow me this Christmas Eve to be allowed
one reprieve.
To see my wife and children this one night; I believe in my heart
this will set things right.
I wanted them to see what you have shown me, but mostly Lord
I want them to believe.
At the end of the prayer God gave the command: Go back down
to this Son of Man,
announce the good news, yes, he can!
The angel woke him in the middle of the night,
announcing the prayer has been answered son of man.
This one thing is done for them, go to your home and give
each one a kiss.
But this will be done while they are snug in their beds,
when they wake in the morning
they will know you were there,
and that this was no dream, a real miracle they will have seen.
So with a swoop and a gasp we suddenly appeared. The first one
I kissed was my littlest dear.
I kissed her forehead like I used to do, saying with all I am,
I love you, be good,
stay safe, and I will always be here. Just know all my days are spent
thinking of you.
My princess was next, so dainty and long. When I kissed her

forehead, she wrinkled her
brow, making me laugh out loud, heart filled with cheer.
I will never be far, and you are always near:
I keep you in my heart forever.
Ahh, their mother, my wife, she's the one who gave me her life.
My beautiful one, my true love, and best friend. I kissed her soft lips and she issued a
sigh. I whispered in her ear: I am, and always will be, in love with her.
I couldn't believe the cascade of tears as I paused for that moment.
I remembered the years—
it truly is such a selfish thing to think that your choices affect only you.
The truth is you are not your own. You belong to everyone.
We returned just like that as I choked back the tears,
remembering my family filled me with cheer.
Thank you, Lord, for all the memories, blessings, and your guiding light, for giving me my my family,
if only for this one night.
When you all awake in this morning light, just know I was with you and kissed you all goodnight.

EDWIN CRUZ

Thoughts

Sitting in a 9 x 6 box, no metal bars—
just automatic doors and concrete walls.
Living in a system where we're constantly put down;
it's hard to stand tall.
I'm surrounded negative influences, drug addicts, and cowards.
How are we expected to strive?
Like animals all we think about is survive.
Damn—how did *I* get here?
My tolerance, patience, and talents being wasted—
it's hard to move ahead when we're blinded hatred.
Yet the parole board expects and demands I persevere...
believe me, my desires of rehabilitation are real.
But realistic expectations diminish my hope.
Misplaced loyalty and dreams distorted dope.
Shattered promises, all this shit is a gimmick.
When I hear politicians speak, I hope they choke!
Man, this whole situation is surreal.
Every day I pinch myself to remind me it's real.

KORY DARTY

Beyond the Mask

MY APPEARANCE and my inner being have been battling with each other for years in the shadow of my soul. For much in my life, appearance claimed victory. "Excuse me sir," people would say. "Your teeth are so white and look at that big beautiful smile!"

It was a victory that felt so good I desperately tried to magnify my self-esteem through it, not realizing I was just covering up the wounds from being burned in the fire of pain. I dressed up the carrying case of my soul in the latest designer fashions. A dab of Cool Water cologne made me feel strong like Mr. Smooth and Paul Bunyan. A finger-wave do in my hair, and a pep in my step, I turned my hat to an angle and looked like I'd just walked out of a Hollywood movie. But inside, my being was starved for attention like a runaway child.

What happened? I was acting out of my own insecurities. I was basing myself on what or who I let get close to my heart and hurt it. Because of years of those dysfunctional, traumatized relationships I tried to save the same people that kept pushing my soul under drowning water. I questioned my own goodness and learned how to hide my true essence. I jumped off the porch of love like a bad habit. Mr. Con Artist became a drug of choice. Peter-Paying-Paul was my handle. The habitat of my life was filled with cockroaches and rats running in and out of deathtraps.

I was standing outside of my body, trying to find a way back in. I spent years knocking on the doors of reality. I am the only son that kept tears swimming on my parents' faces. I was the brother that stepped back from the plate. I dealt many friendships a black eye. I danced with the devil like I was on death row, waiting for that envelope to surrender my life.

One day while relaxing in the sensualities of my fleshly desires, a question crossed my mind like breaking news: Kory Latrell Darty—what's your purpose in life? From that day forward, I put my character, morals, and goals on trial. I became the co-judge of my identity as I weighed all the evidence. My verdict: The Bible was right. Pride did come before my fall.

The Holy Spirit then helped me draw answers from my spiritual awakening so I could align my internal person at heart with my external appearance. I learned how to address how I feel. I asked myself, why do I let emotions dictate my true being? I became aware that feelings don't have wisdom, intellect, free will, or choice—but I do. This helped the outcome of how I carry myself today, with respect, veneration, and solidarity. Now I smile on the outside because I'm smiling on the inside—my inner experience of peace comes from my true nature.

CHRISTIAN DIAZ

Fated to Be Destined to Shape

Fate decrees all that is and all that is to be.
Destiny not chained to fate, announces what it shapes.
Fate inscribed the Law of Death, expressed in every breath.
Destiny shaped the art of will when intentions manifest.

Fate declares to me from day to day, that I will surely die.
Destiny assures me my soul ascends this life.

I cursed Fate night and day for the things I have to be.
I asked Fate, what's the use of a life without eternity?
I asked Fate, what's the use of birth, when death's the final curse?
What's the use of love when evil men demand your blood?
What's the use of joy when pain comes to destroy?

Fate remains silent to my curses, so destiny steps in.
Destiny starts singing happy songs of things that surely end.
Destiny writes me poems of broken hearts to be amended.
Destiny shapes great works of art to be enjoyed and not contended.

Destiny declares to me, "oh, you foolish soul!"
It's not about what comes and goes or what will not remain.
Do flowers bloom in deserts if they're not nourished with rain?
Can children be conceived if a mother's not of age?
Can fire keep you warm without the branch to feed the flame?

Something must be given up for something else to change.
Without the special giving that's a beautiful exchange.
Nothing in existence will ever reach a higher stage.

The seed must die and shed its shell for the flower to arise.
Father heaven must release his tears for Mother Earth to stay alive.
A girl must grow to womanhood to conceive another life.

The branch dies to the flame to keep you warm throughout the night.

Through all this giving and exchanging there's no such thing as loss.
There's no such thing as forever, no such thing as cost.
Just appreciation for what is, and appreciation for what's not.
Appreciate this wisdom that your heart has really sought.

Apologize to Fate, for that's all she has to be
She's the one that keeps things grounded for all that is to be.
That doesn't mean you're alone, without a destiny.
For the power of your will can shape your whole reality.
For destiny is shaped and Fate decrees to be.
But there's nothing more important than the moment we breathe.

CHRISTIAN DIAZ

Face & Heart

FACE AND HEART—an Aztec expression—represents the dual character of existence. Face is the surface of everything that can be seen in life, while Heart is the unseen root below the surface.

As long as the root is deep, what springs to the surface can truly never perish. One is the reflection of the other.

The ancient expression of "Face and Heart" is easily understood when one observes human relations. Face is what can obviously be observed, such as speech, actions, reactions, and body language. Heart is less obvious, hidden from view, such beliefs, perceptions, feelings and life experiences.

As can be seen, the Face aspect of humans (speech, actions, reactions and body language) are a direct reflection of the Heart aspect (beliefs, perceptions, feelings, and life experiences).

Speech reflects belief. You speak to express your belief. Body language reflects feelings; the way the body speaks reveals what it feels. Actions reflect perceptions; you act on how you perceive things. Reactions reflect life experiences; you react to situations based on experiences that life has dealt you in the past.

The expression of Face and Heart is as relevant today as it was in the ancient Aztec era. This wise expression teaches us that the face you present the world, should also represent and reflect the inner world of the heart. And that reflection should be rooted in purity. The root is the purity of love. The nurturing soil is the uncontaminated Heart, the center of our being, in which all things springs forth. And then wisdom is what blossoms in the Face.

TUAN "MIKE" DOAN

Be Still

THE HEAVY metal door rattled as the mechanical chain pulled it open. The loud noise was like a speaker announcing to those inside of a new arrival. I straightened my back, puffed out my chest. My face changed, masking my nervousness. With an uneasy step, I entered the pod, looking like a lost confused boy who had walked into a classroom full of strangers on his first day at a new school. Their eyes, cold, stared from behind the narrow Plexiglas window of their cells. They pierced into me like curious predators wondering who I am, friend or foe, and why I am here. My eyes met theirs, but only for a split second. I gave each a polite nod to acknowledge them as two correctional officers escorted me down the hall to the opened cell at the far end.

At the sight of the Correctional Officers (COs), a wild-eyed inmate began to shout out a litany of complaints and accusations. "You are holding my mail. I know it. Don't play games with me. You assholes turned down the pressure on my sink. I know it. There's no hot water. So that's how you guys want to play, huh? Well suckers, I wrote to the President of the U.S. of A." He dragged out the letter. "He's going to send his people down here to check you fools. Watch! They're gonna come... FBI succa. The badges is gonna shine all up ya faces." He went on and on with his mindless statements, sounding more and more like a J-cat (crazy). The COs ignored him. I did too.

My heart raced as I entered my 6-by-8-foot cell that felt like a concrete tomb, no bigger than the bathroom of an average size home. The heavy door closed behind me, locking me inside this gray enclosed tomb with a loud clang. I began to feel claustrophobic, drowned in the emptiness of the tiny cell.

I took in a needed breath and let out a calming sigh, hoping it would slow the anxieties that had begun to sweep over me.

"You'll get used to it. Things will get better," I tried comforting myself, but the feeling of despair and loneliness wouldn't allow comforting words to register in my mind. It felt as though there was a tug of war being fought between my analytical mind and my loud emotions. Each had its reason that the other stubbornly refused to accept. I felt tired, mentally drained. All I wanted was to lie down and sleep, to forget about this place, forget I once again had been herded like cattle to a new farm.

I lazily walked over to the metal locker and removed the things I'd been holding from a plastic bag: a small plastic spoon, a roll of toilet paper, half a bar of soap, a two-inch toothbrush, and a paper cup with tooth powder sitting at the bottom. I laid everything neatly inside the locker then turned around to my concrete bed where an old worn mattress laid on top. Its insides spilled loosely out of the holes some inmate had tried desperately to patch up.

I removed one of the two clean, but just as worn, sheets lying on top of the mattress and hastily made my bed. I fell onto the bed, pulling the extra sheet over my head. I closed my eyes, pretending I was home in my comfortable bed with mom in the kitchen preparing a wonderful thanksgiving meal, the turkey perfectly glazed with my mom's secret sauce, its juicy aroma filling every room of the house. My stomach growled at the thought. I pushed the thought aside, not further teasing my empty stomach, and tried to sleep. But sleep was impossible on the thin lumpy mattress.

I tossed and turned trying desperately to find a decent spot, which couldn't be done. I curled into a fetal position, my hands tucked between my legs, cocooned underneath my sheet, listening to the wheezing vent blowing out cold air. The air so cold my teeth chattered, my body shivered uncontrollably in my white boxers and t-shirt.

Unable to sleep, I got up. I wrapped the sheet around my shoulder and paced the room, taking five quick steps, spinning around, and marching back. Back and forth I went, trying to keep warm with the repetitious movement to nowhere.

Boredom began to toy with my restless mind, forcing me to find ways to entertain myself. My eyes scanned the room, reading graffiti that inmates had written or scratches on walls, locker and door. Most of the graffiti was gang related, proudly displaying their alias and neighborhoods. But some were private thoughts. "Jenny, I love you" was printed neatly in pencil on the wall. The writer of the message remained anonymous, too ashamed of his foolish moment of amorousness to take claim. An innocent display of affection in a hostile environment could be perceived as a sign of weakness. "Too young to die, too proud to cry," was lazily scribbled on the side of the locker Mr. Smurf. "John 3:16" was etched into the door.

After I was bored reading graffiti, I found new ways to entertain myself. I began to look for small holes and cracks in the walls. Two holes and a long crack in the middle became Mickey Mouse. But on further and careful inspection, I declared it to be Dumbo with his big ears and long nose. And on I went giving each notable combination of cracks and holes an identity. But after a while, this too no longer entertained my quickly bored mind. And in no time, boredom was like a leaking faucet, so palpable in its tiny endless drops.

Unanswered questions about this place raced through my mind. Maybe I should ask my neighbor, I suggested to myself. No, I shouldn't. He didn't look too friendly standing behind the thick Plexiglas window, eyeing me with his tattooed chest like a billboard proudly advertising his neighborhood in big black letters. He might be another J-cat. But maybe he might not be, I painfully debated with myself. With dreaded heart, I hesitantly stepped onto the toilet, but shyly jumped back down. Go ahead, talk to him, the voice inside of me encouraged. Reluctantly, I stepped back onto the toilet, my face pressed close to the vent. "Excuse me neighbor," I called out above the wheezing vent, keeping the tone in my voice level.

"What's up?" a voice rang out from the other side. I could hear a foot climbing on top of the stainless-steel toilet on the other side. I politely told him my name, my ethnicity, and why I was here. He in turn did the same, with pleasantness in his voice that made my heart smile.

He gave me a succinct rundown of the program: "Shower every other day for five minutes, except Wednesday; laundry once a week on Thursday; no yard, no book–don't bother to ask. Make sure you ask for two blankets and a towel after dinner–that you could ask for."

I was given a heads-up not to entertain the inmate who had shouted out at the COs with conversation. "He's a crazy," my neighbor warned. I already figured he was. "That dude's been in here for over two years. They said he attacked a CO who was talking shit to him." He was cool the first year, but now... man, he yelled and talked shit to everyone. They tried forcing him to take his pill but he refused."

After answering the rest of my inquiries, my neighbor kindly asked if I wanted to check out a book. "Yeah, of course," I wanted to shout. A book to me in a place where the only form of entertainment was staring at the walls or daydreaming was priceless. I would even trade my breakfast for a book. If it's a really good book, I'll even throw in my sack lunch. "Yeah, if you could spare one," I coolly replied.

A minute later, a fishing line torn from a sheet with a mustard pack tied to the end slid in front of my door. "Go ahead and pull two times on the line," he instructed. I stuck my fingers underneath the bottom crack and pulled on the line. I brought in a book split in half to fit underneath my door. I couldn't believe it. A Western! My favorite. A giddy smile spread over my face. The book he loaned was clenched tightly in my hand.

The days, weeks, and months that followed our first meeting were quite interesting. The two of us, once complete strangers, separated a thick wall that made us feel like we were a continent apart, now quickly bonded. This forged into an endearing friendship the loneliness and boredom of this miserable place.

We spent our days passing time working out. At night we stood on our toilet, our faces pressed inches from the vent so we could hear each other over the wheezing sound. Our faces ached from the cold air, but we didn't mind. We were just glad to be entertained each other's stories about ourselves, our family, our girlfriend, our ex's, our hopes and our dreams.

We were two men from different cultures and different upbringing, but when we shared about our family, our shame and guilt were tangible to the other. We described how sad it was we had let our families down, especially our mothers, to whose endless love and encouragement we had failed to listen.

We talked about letting go of our past and starting anew, never forgetting our bad choices, but also never letting them define who we are or who we desire to become better human beings.

Twice a week, mostly on weekends, we declared an hour of karaoke night. That hour we sang whatever we wanted. Madonna's "Like a Virgin" got a little play. And mostly due to my unyielding encouragement, my somewhat shy neighbor would always kick it off. He sang off-key and often with missing lyrics. I would grin and painfully hold back the laughter that was itching to burst through my throat. I was always kind in giving him praise, even suggesting he could go on *American Idol* and possibly win. He laughed. I laughed.

When it was my turn, I sang with all my passion and soul as though I was singing in front of thousands, not just one. And, no matter how dreadful my singing was, my neighbor was quick to shower me with compliments. I smiled at his kind words, but knew quite well that, on the other side of the wall, a big grin was spreading over his face.

Time flew as we continued to find new ways to entertain ourselves in the hole. Our corny jokes were so lame we had to laugh. But everything changes, and time seemed to be at a standstill for me the day he got word he was transferring. We said our goodbyes, wishing each other a safe and better journey in life. That night again I felt alone and overwhelmed with the silence, except for the wheezing vent. I laid on my bed and read the last chapter of the book I had been saving just for a moment like this. I put it down beside me after I had finished reading it, quite upset at myself for reading it so fast. My eyes stared blankly into the room. My mind zoned out with thoughts of lonely days ahead.

I thought about my neighbor and one of the stories he had shared. A thin smile spread over my face. "Man, when I was young, every time I got in trouble and my mom spanked me, I would wail and cry, pretending it hurt. She would feel guilty and stop." He laughed a hearty laughter full of boyish innocence. "Man, this always worked," he declared pertly, paused, and then added with a profound sincerity: "Man, I love her."

My eyes, lost in a trance, stared at the dim glow from the yellow light above my sink. A barely legible writing above the sink caught my eyes. I wondered how I'd missed it. I squinted my eyes, too lazy to get up, and read it. I read it again, slowly. I closed my eyes, allowing the words to sink into my heart. My feeling of despair and loneliness began to lift from my heart, and in its place were feelings of gratitude and appreciation. My mind, for the first time since I've been here, became still.

I opened my eyes and looked around at my surroundings, grateful to have a roof over my head, clothes to wear, and three meals a day. I spoke softly the words on the wall, filling the empty silence with its touching message: "I complained because I have no shoes, then I met a man who had no feet."

Thy soul shall find itself alone
'Mid dark thoughts of the gray tombstone–
Not one of the crowd to pry
Into thine hour of secrecy.
Be silent in that solitude,
Which is not loneliness, for then
The spirit of the dead who stood
In life before thee, on their will
Shall overshadow thee:
Be still.

(From the book Gemini Man)

TUAN "MIKE" DOAN

I Am a Man

HIS EYES closed, he rocked gently back and forth in his wooden rocker, taking in the cool breeze of an early spring morning. He could hear the gentle wind, laughing, toying with the leaves from an oak tree, blowing branches one way then another. Sparrows and finches chirped loudly with excitement, hopping from branch to branch, chasing away unwanted visitors from newly claimed territory. A bee buzzed around the old man. He was tempted to chase it away with his hand but decided to let it be and hope it will go on with its business and leave him alone. After a few seconds the bee flew away, probably to the flowers that had sprouted out from the once frozen ground.

The sound of nature full of life danced around him, relaxing his body and sending his silent thoughts back to the never forgotten past, forcing him to conjure images that had long ago been ingrained in the back of consciousness. He wished the images weren't there, but they were. He had resigned to the fact they would always be there, be part of him. He had tried pushing them back, way back, but stubbornly the images refused to obey and slowly drifted into his thoughts, dwelling in his mind until he could no longer resist their unwanted visits. And once again, he painfully gave in.

"You're just a monkey boy," the kid in his school had teased. "Go back to where you came from, monkey boy." "Monkey boy! Monkey boy!" they shouted in unison. Their taunting words coursed through his veins, on fire. These words inched closer to his heart, poisoning it with each painful breath he took. His tiny chest heaved heavily, begging for the cool air to fill his aching lungs and slow the pounding in his heart, which he was afraid would explode and kill him. Maybe it would be best if it did explode, he silently thought. That way he wouldn't be around for them to tease.

Dejected and alone, he painfully walked away. His feet began to move faster and faster, taking him further and further away from his tormentors. His feet pounded on the dirt path that led to his home.

He quickly dashed inside, headed straight for the bathroom. Staring at himself in the mirror, he angrily brushed the shameful tears that had streaked down his face. He picked up a wooden brush and tried to straighten out his nappy hair, wishing it wasn't so nappy, for that's what the kids in school had called it. Frustrated that all his attempts were in vain, he took a clipper and shaved it all off. He looked at himself in the mirror. For a split second his chest was no longer crushing him. He took in an easy breath. No longer a nappy head. At that moment, he didn't' care if his mom would be disappointed what he did. He had his reasons and she couldn't understand. They didn't make fun of *her*. They didn't laugh at and taunt her.

He knew his mom would try to comfort him. Like many other times she would speak with gentle encouragement, "Son, let Jesus guide your heart and let hope fill your mind." Her kind words, and unconditional love for him, only brushed at his heart. At that time, they hardly registered to his 7-year-old mind.

He wished he was no longer a boy but a man—a big strong man, so big no one would dare tease him. And if they did, he would send his fists into them with a grievance they would understand and remember. For it was his right to be a man.

The old man slowly opened his wise old eyes and they were wet. A tear had escaped the corner of his eyes and streaked down his face. He thought about his mom, how wise and loving she was to him and those around her. He wished he could go back in time and shake the youthful ignorance he had allowed to fill his heart with false pride, a foolish pride that had chained him down, refusing to let him become a good man like his mother had envisioned and prayed for. No! He was a fool who lost twenty good years of his life behind bars, a concrete tomb he had called home.

The old man sadly shook his pepper gray hair. He took a deep breath, let out a long sigh to gather himself before getting up. He strolled over to the garden. He bent down, his back like a crescent moon, and began pulling out weeds that had crept in around his flowers. In the short distance, he could see little Tim walking to school, his blonde hair lightly tossing in the wind. A good boy. Little Tim waved his hand at the old man. The old man straightened his body; once again he felt big and strong. He gave the little boy a warm smile and returned the wave.

FORRREST GREEN

The Ifs in Love

If there is love:
Are the boundaries firmly set into place?
Or do they shift constantly at a regular pace?

If there is love:
How much will I get when willing to pay?
And if I'm not satisfied, am I permitted to say?

If there is love:
What are the conditions I must first comprehend?
If we don't agree, are there any I'm authorized to amend?

If there is love:
What quantity do I receive if ever you realize we're indigent?
Does it really matter, or will it cease, after all our capital's been spent?

If there is love:
Does it tend to increase as long as I am considerate?
Or like the ebb and flow of the ocean, does it fluctuate?

If there is love:
Where is the definite limit I may push to?
And do the restrictions set for me, also apply to you?

If there is love:
Will it diminish if I become detrimental to myself and others?
Or possibly evaporate completely with the feeling you're wasting time, so why bother?

The answer to these questions is void or "D" for *None of the Above*.
Because when it is true, there is absolutely no... *if* in love.

FORREST GREEN

Color of Betrayal

The betrayal I encountered had the feeling of the red heat
from an iron, branded onto my heart.

The deception was genius, brilliantly performed out in plain sight,
with the coolness of blue arctic ice.

My green-eyed intuition tried to warn me,
   but I was stubbornly in denial.
All the way up until it was no longer in dispute and staring me
   defiantly in the face.

With the feeling of somehow being the blame, I was plunged
   into that gray area
of indecision, wondering if I should hold on, just let go.

Realizing the level of betrayal heaped upon me could never have been
   my own doing,
I was swallowed the black of despair. Curious as to what more
   I could've done.

Deprived of that which was so prevalent to me,
   my life is reduced to mere existence
in a purple haze. Hoping someday the fog will lift,
   imparting a clear understanding.

I seek and search, but still wonder how I could be so
   deaf, dumb, and blind.
And with that thought, I am wounded
   with the white pain of my retrospection.

DONTAY USHAWN HAYES

Initiations

Initiations...
From the beginning of age
recorded and written,
boys have become men
through rites of initiation.
Age fluctuates as the end becomes beginning.
13 is the age most men enter
at least in the tribes I've seen,
in the communities where I've been
where death and drugs most often determine.
A select few make it through
their rites in the fight,
on the field, court, or in the booth
spitting power to truth.
Not much realizing when you do.
The powers that be still buy, trade, and sell you.
Shackled, no breakthroughs in the rituals through which
they initiate you.
On the flipside, imagine if you and I
sat and said: if you want to be an *ese*, Blood, Crip, up north, down
south, or not affiliate, to be a part of this you must commit
to what you've missed...
What sets you apart because a true
community has specialists in every field.
So produce what you have
and together we will create a better path
away from graveyards and prison yards
and produce a world of spiritually
decent moral children.
Let initiated-beginning begin
where foes become friends,
hate becomes love,

and enough to eat for all can be the new drug of choice.
This is just the world I'd love to see initiated,
expressed in my voice.

DONTAY DUSHAWN HAYES

Don't Change the Direction, Direct the Change

Balance the rage.
Balance the dark matter and naivety.
Balance the perception of reality dreams.
Focus, now pay attention...
Everything isn't what it seems.
To create what for you is most important,
          be determined and willing to navigate
          through something foreign
          unbeknown!
          unfamiliar, completely new.
The terrain is territory when viewed
          as something to do.
The people, family, friends, allies,
through thick and thin.
The obligation, to differentiate
          those who pretend from those who really want to win...
          then the planning can begin
The goals on paper mapped out
          like a mission statement.
Headed to that destination
          designated for me
          and patiently waiting
          for my arrival...
Each and every one of us
          exploring our genius key to survival.

DONTAY DUSHAWN HAYES

Keep Walking

Each step,
each breath,
each challenge,
every time you've doubted...
You are a part of a plan,
piece to a puzzle
you may never understand.
When your feet are heavy
and weighted down
your mind,
keep walking.
keep stepping,
even when you are crying inside,
trying to hide
the fact you wanna die...
When you wish you did not exist,
and everyone and everything
seems to be against you.
Alone you pray.
God will fix you!
And have a hand in all you do
that it was anybody but you
going through what it is you are going through...
Keep walking,
keep stepping,
keep inflecting
till you find the direction.
You will know
this is the way
you should be headed,
just keep stepping,
keep walking.

SPOON JACKSON

Calm

Most people shy away,
and not towards,
a storm.
Most people back away,
and not try to ride
a tidal wave.

But there is a calm
at the heart of a storm,
sometimes peaceful and warm.
I long to step
into the tranquility,
the silence of a hurricane
where cherry blossoms form.

No bickering, no hatred,
no bullying, and no lies.
Just calm in the midst of chaos.

There must be untold
light there,
a slumbering goddess,
where kindness flourish
and one can leave
this world behind.

SPOON JACKSON

Heal

Like a heart
that keeps giving,
I must keep believing
in the power of healing.

Sometimes I grind
down so hard on my teeth
I crack them during sleep:
I must wear a tooth guard at night.

Sometimes a long deep
cry alone, or with a loved one,
will open your eyes, your heart,
to the power of healing.

Like a heart
that keeps giving,
I must keep believing
in the powers of healing.

Sometimes just a smile,
a hug, a kiss, or hello
will heal the soul.

Sometimes a book, a letter,
a song, a poem, a dream,
or loss of a loved one,
will open your eyes, your heart,
to the power of healing.

Sometimes a long silence,
solitude, a tree, a meadow,

a long howl,
or swallow's song,
will open your eyes, your heart
to the power of healing.

I don't know what
or who I have not forgiven.
And I know there's
something that needs healing
like a heart that keeps giving.

I must keep believing,
I must keep believing,
in the power of healing.

SEAN KELLY

Me

I'm losing my mind–
weeks, months, years go by,
but I'm frozen in time.
Crying, praying, hoping,
living a nightmare but somehow
my eyes are open.
Mad, sad, and angry while
my friends are out laughin' and joking'.
Incarcerated, isolated, segregated–
physically fit
but mentally whipped.
Gagged and bound,
crying on the inside, but not a tear falls down.
If this were my path, then, Lord, take me now.
Suicidal, at times homicidal,
trying to fix this broken soul is like
solving a puzzle
with no fingers and blindfolded.
In these few lines is my heart unfolded–
don't enclose it,
but hold it
in your mind
so you know what's in mine.
Very few can see
but now you can actually say
you know me.

JIMMY MCMILLAN

Poem Cry

I can't see 'em coming down my eye,
so I had to make this poem cry,
this pen bleed,
this paper scream with emotions with hopes it makes
us free...
Can you relate to feeling faceless in a sea of faces?
No more than a nomad on a path that went nowhere fast.
Cuz we're still judged the deeds of our past...
What does the future hold?
When our presence is evident in every element,
and they tell us as long as we in prison, we irrelevant.
Cuz it's hard to bloom on these crowded rooms where it's
often dark–
And searching for light can take a lifetime–
if ya lost ya spark.
Lost in thought, so I often thought I couldn't smile.
For my inner child–*What-up lil homie?*–it's been awhile.
You are seen. Like the vestige of a dream.
Where every deed is magnified like the ripples in a stream,
and it seems we've seen so many nightmare scenes,
that it doesn't take a horror to make us scream.
Holla!
Pain is love–and it's a thin line between that and hate.
And it's not too late to be strong enough to subtract the hate.
Long as you add the love–give everything you have to
Love–and ya house of healing becomes a house of love.
And that's what's up! I couldn't see 'em coming down my eye,
so I had to make this poem cry.

JIMMY MCMILLAN

The Fog

Drifting in the distance,
I try to move through these cluttered views,
constantly reminded
of the times I got lost in this crimson haze,
feeling like I'm in a daze
or trapped in a maze.
I'm inside a nightmare, and when I wake up
I realize I'm just in a cage.
So I lash out–
hoping I ain't the 'last out" in the Game of Judges.
I hold grudges
as well as stones in my glass house.
This... red mist
consists of a clenched fist,
and it's hard to tell
if I'm off the rails,
off the tracks
when it seems, this fog is back,
bitter cold, feeling numb, got the chill in my soul.
Too young to be feeling so old.
White shoals in these shallow waters,
melancholy mood got me consumed in these dark rooms.
Time is flawed in the white fog.
Darkness is my doctrine.
I'm a scholar when the lights are off.
They say the devil's in the details,
the framework of a black mist.
My future is past tense.
I move through these dark hues,
trying to change my color scheme to light greens and blues.
Let the sunshine thru.
Evaporate this mist with a gift,

something I ain't had in a while...
a smile.

JIMMY MCMILLAN

Justice

Is it justice or Just-us?
I can't tell. Nor can I ignore the war that has been waged on the poor,
the disgruntled, the shrinking middle class, the immigrants,
the 99 percent that don't pay rent in Manhattan's sky rises
and the high rise in cost of living, not to mention all
the men & women lost to prisons.
Code Red...
It's a new type of domestic terrorism,
the type that rip hope from your Federal Reserve Notes.
Quotes from old masters can no longer capture
the essence of life's lessons.

It used to take a village—
now technology raises the children.
Media move us like puppets in this new republic.
I am everyday people, but I don't need the social network,
to tell me my net worth.
My days on this earth has been compounded this hard life
and hard living
that we are all living.
And I don't apologize for this God giving that I'm giving.
So check the revelation...
Ya government bailout could have gave the whole U.S. reparations.
Instead you took a chainsaw to education and sliced the knowledge
and raised the price on college...
Or so I hear.
And even hear behind closed doors a cold world is still a frigid
existence.
And even in the pen, my pen can lead the resistance.
But they want us on both sides like division:
Divide and conquer.
And if that don't work, they'll throw some dope at us and see who

goes for the contra.
In contrast, you won't need Comcast to see the Bombast.
They just waiting on the aftermath.
And I don't need a donkey to tell me how to act an ass.
Something's gotta give.
Don't apologize for being rich, but don't tell the rest how to live.
There is no such thing as social equality in a Democracy,
only economics and commerce that's capitalism.
And no activism can stop the machine.
That's why all the rest of companies, um I mean countries,
adopt the regime.
Even those with Kings & Queens.

Justice isn't blind,
she's just for sale.
And the veil fell from her eyes soon as she tilted her scales.
They close the borders in this New World Order,
cause it don't make cents to give quarters.
This aint for the faint hearted.
We are gathered here today to mourn our dearly departed...
Her name is Justice,
and she Just left and left Just us.

TONY MORENO

The Mexican Revolution

The Mexican Revolution might have begun with Miguel Hidalgo,
but it finished with real Revolutionary masters.
Hidalgo fought the Spanish crown, however Zapata and Villa
emerged as sincere Mexican Idols.
With every odd against them, they fought
for Land and Liberty,
placing all their faith in their belief but also on much
of the peasantry.
Not enough credit is given to the females who choose to fight
alongside these soldiers who stood the tallest.
So I would love to salute Emiliano Zapata, Francisco Villa,
and the Infamous *Maria Pistolas* with this homage.

DAMON MULLIN

Fate & Destiny

Fate & Destiny, two sides of the same coin, yet varied in their functions.

Life & Death, the other inseparable aspects of the coin.

One can argue that fate & destiny are different, but for one who views reality from the lens of there being no coincidence in life, that there is no mere chance or happenstance, or that possibilities can or will be whatever they happen to be.

Good fortune gained no matter how attained isn't fortuitous or serendipitous simply because you did not anticipate its arrival.

Nor is fate inseparable from destiny. It is one's fate that determines one's destiny—how far the bowstring is drawn determines how far the arrow will go.

Destiny is that arrow that arises from fate's wings and its trajectory is what erases the thin veil that distinguishes destiny & fate.

Ponder if you will: fate & destiny are just impressions on either side of the coin; remove the impressions the coin remains.

A blank canvas destined to be what its possessor desires it to be, fated to be simply what it is.

DANIEL (CRAZY MINDED) NEWMAN

When the streetlamps come on

When the streetlamps come on, it's time to go in.
Our parents didn't want us in the dangers of the night.
During the nighttime is when it all begins.
Illegal activity, "Ding!" goes the light.
I call two people, it's just me and my friends.
Strolling through the hood, also known as the Trailer Park.
Tagging on the walls–cans, markers, and pens.
Feeling like we're bad asses, unseen through the dark.
Dressed in all black, in the darkness we blend.
I and Spooky have knives, Demon has the strap.
Each one of us fearless, so we pretend.
A random man approaches so Demon busted a cap.
A loud crack, the guy falls, and we turn the bend.
Everything goes fast, my mind can't think.
Suddenly the hood becomes unknown, like a fen.
Looking down the street, it all starts to shrink.
Sirens in the distance, thinking this is the end.
I tell the homies "Let's get back to the pad."
We stash the strap and get home right at ten.
As we get to the door, it opens and there stands my dad.
Disappointment on his face he said the word "Again?"
Unable to speak, no words come to mind.
Glancing up and down, asking himself "Why him?"
A fucked up feeling is the only thing I could find.
When the streetlamps come on, it's time to stay in.

DANIEL (CRAZY MINDED) NEWMAN

Realization

A bright light flashes.
The window crashes.
I'm wide awake and shivering cold, feeling groggy–
then BAM! I get hit but feel no pain.
Dazed and confused, says my brain,
It's a flashback but I'm not in my body–
I'm staring at myself through someone else's eyes.
Hot Cheetos on the floor, anger on his face, tears falling, I guess I cry.
A few seconds pass, I realize I'm my wife, and the room gets foggy–
now I'm outside, it's wet and chilly.
Walking down the street contemplating if he's going to kill me.
It all starts to slip away into a helicopter view, vision godly.

A bright light flashes.
The window crashes.
I'm at home cleaning up some chips, feeling filthy–
then BAM! The realization hits me.
I just experienced what my wife went through with me;
drop to my knees, eyes flooding, I'm feeling guilty.
How can I do this to the woman of my dreams,
over something so petty as who's her favorite team?
All because we were drinking, my thoughts are all negative, oddly–
we're both Reds fans but this night she was claiming Dodgers.
Wish I could take it all back and apologize, but why bother?
The dream evaporates. I wake up to realize...
about me there's nothing godly.

ERIC L. "JALIL" NICHOLSON

The Greatest Love I Know

The sound of rain reminds me of our distance
as we share the loneliness and experience the pain.
With memories flowing clear, my heart skips a beat,
a tear falls from my eye, as I embrace the warmth,
while holding you near.
Feeling the pleasure as well as the pain,
suffering your precious lost with nothing left to gain.
They say you reap what you sow, I can agree that much,
living life without your smile, your smell, your soft touch.
I would give anything to awake your side,
though I failed in my past, the truth I cannot hide.
I've come to realize you reap what you sow,
meaning you plant the seeds of love and watch them grow.
My bad choices are the fruit through the work I wrought,
though my intentions were good, it is only pain I brought.
Now I sit with nothing more than a dream, a sigh, a silent cry,
I'll always love you until the day I die.
Here's hugs, love, and kisses in case you didn't know,
you are my one desire, the greatest love I'll ever know.

ERIC L. "JALIL" NICHOLSON

Sing of Truth

Sing a song of truth,
sing proud and strong,
sing for the old and new,
sing of me, sing of you.
Sing that all may hear
of struggles of the past,
sing your message through.
Sing for the weak and the strong,
sing loud and true.
Sing away the pain,
sing for hope and joy.
Sing for our nation,
every man, woman, girl, and boy.
Sing for the lost, and remember the dead,
as we sing of the grind and getting ahead.
Sing of our soul,
sing of our faith,
sing of our hope,
sing of our grace.
Sing to smile,
sing to cry,
sing from our birth,
until our time to die.
Sing for love,
sing for self,
sing for the memories
of our cultural wealth.
Sing for the glory
still locked inside,
regardless of the history
they tried to hide.

Lift your voices
in one regard
so the world may once again
feel the presence of God.
Sing, sing, sing of me, sing of you.

DANIEL LINO ONOPA

Red, White, and Black Fogs

"Blind Rage and Anger"
Red Fog

One night, in a drunken stupor, I lost my car keys. My companion and I were forced to get to our final destination on our legs, which wasn't walking distance. As drunk and tired as we were, it was also late, so when we saw someone coming over the hill on a bike, the only thing I saw in my mind was wheels. Wheels turned into "Where you from?" "Where you from" turned into "now that we got our transportation, what else you got?" If I remember correctly, he had a cell phone and exactly five dollars. What's humorously ironic about this is that on my hip I had a Blackberry of my own and in my pocket I had at least $3,000—enough money to buy 15 of his phones. But when it's late and you're intoxicated, all necessary reasoning goes out the window. So, when the judge slammed his gavel, along came the fogs and the proverbial "fuck-it" button was pushed. I called this time in 2008 "My Red Fog"; I believe it hit me the hardest when I was sentenced to 22 years for a cellphone and five dollars.

"Numbness and Haziness"
White Fog

The problem with hitting the fuck-it button is that your pride and frustration won't allow you to "un-hit" it! Not that it can't be undone, but you get this tick in your mind that tells you that humility at this point is irrelevant, so *no mas dale*. Inevitably, I ended up in the Segregated Housing Unit (SHU) because my recklessness got me into some real ugly ordeals. Most inmates utilize their first few months to reevaluate their lives and/or situations depending on the nature of the act. Most take this time to sit and think—think about the "how's" and the "why's" and the "what now's?" For me, in my first few months, my girlfriend called it quits, my cousin passed away along with my grandmother, and a month later her husband, my grandfather, joined her. Add all these stressful events to my already rage-filled numbness, and I reached my tipping point into the abyss.

"Suicide"
Black Fog

I remember cutting everyone out of my life. Family, friends... everyone. They would write me, and I would read their letters, but I wouldn't respond to them. Concerned, they even tried to get my ex-girlfriend to send me a letter to see where my mind was at. But I wouldn't respond. The money kept coming and I didn't send them so much as a thank you. Don't get it twisted—I didn't check out to where I couldn't tell the difference between a dream and reality. Fuck that shit. I was as sure as I am now, just didn't give a flying fuck and accepted the fact this is where I was, and this is where I wanted to be. Due to giving a shit less, I finally picked up three more years. I hit the SHU in the beginning of 2011 with 22 years and two strikes as a total term. The end of 2011, I had 25 years and two strikes. I spent four and a half years back there, but two of those years were spent in complete blackness. Eventually I got what I wanted: the letters stopped, and the support was cut super short.

Now the Law of Attraction teaches us that whatever energy you put into the universe, good or bad, you better expect that same energy to come right back. From 2008 to 2011, I gave the universe a full-fledged finger—and for two years in the SHU, the universe shot it right back.

Strength & Courage:
Clearing the Fogs

In 2013, I took a keen notice to this universal reaction, but wasn't yet convinced I needed some order in this messy state of mind I created. After a while of disconnection to the outside world, I became very comfortable with the mailman not stopping at my door. But for the first time in a long time I received a letter, surprisingly, someone I did not know.

She said her name was Lorena and that she found my address from an online pen-pal service. Her letter was sprayed with an intoxicating perfume. With every line I read, I felt like the scent pulled me into a deeper trance. I read that letter 10 or 11 times, before reluctantly I finally responded. My response was brief at first. A quick hello and a thank you for taking the time to reach out to me. Her next letter, and my response, was a little more cordial... a basic introduction from both parties, if you will. The third and the fourth letters, we were sending poetry and pictures to one another, conversing about life and other meaningful intelligent conversations. I remember in one of the connections we spoke of the value of family, how important they are in our lives, and how necessary it is to be in theirs regardless of the circumstance. That's when it hit me—the universe put this brilliant, articulate, and remarkable beautiful being in my path to offer me a better perspective on how to view "my life."

Understanding this new profound gift, but still somewhat fighting it, I remember telling her I had a girlfriend, that we were happy, that I valued our friendship, and that she would have to slow it down before any unnecessary feelings got involved. It took her a while to write back so I thought for sure she would just stop. But, nope, she understood and kept writing. Even if she didn't know I lied to her about the girlfriend, her letters didn't stop. Although she and I didn't know it then, I saw later on that the universe's plan was to slowly dissipate the fogs I've become accustomed to and open up to someone whom I had no prior emotional ties with. A complete stranger.

For the remainder of my time in the SHU, and even to this day, I owe a lot of gratitude to that woman for the huge impact she had on my life. She doesn't write anymore, and I'm fine with that. It's been almost four years now, and as we inmates know all too well, time takes its toll. Nevertheless, even though I didn't know it then, I sought help, stayed focused, and found my purpose in life. I own my life now and have for quite some time, but had it not been for the SHU, that individual in my life, and the circumstances I've experienced, I wouldn't be the man whom you sit with today.

DANIEL LINO ONOPA

If I Was an Instrument

I unzip the case that's held me dust-free for years. Inside this huge instrument made of cherry wood and nylon strings is a symbol of who I am and what I've become. But I can't just be released from my tomb and expect to make beautiful music without first giving myself the proper tuning.

Where's my bow? I can't find my bow. Without it I can't figure out what parts of me need adjustments. Where's that damn thing at? Now I'm getting frustrated. Well I'll set up first and maybe I'll find it. I unfasten the leg that keeps me grounded and place it into one of these carved holes of the base on the floor. This leg represents my morals and strong character and without it I couldn't stand at all.

I still can't find my bow, but let's see how this family chord sounds if I pluck at it a few times. Nah, that's not right. What about my religion chord? Same thing. I would try my *arte* chord, but I know I don't need tuning there because I got that down pat. The only chord that's left is my *emotions*. Let's see, maybe like my *arte* chord, it won't need tuning. I pluck at my *arte* chord just to see if I'm tripping. Damn it! All these chords sound the same. Where the hell is that bow? Now I'm pissed.

Aww, there it is—underneath my anger and frustration. I forget that sometimes when I'm mad, I can't see what's right in front of me. Oblivious to all else that's important. So, I take a deep breath, release that negative energy, and tighten up my bow.

With the first strike at my family chord, I can hear immediately the sound isn't the right pitch. A few turns of the knob and I'm back on track. I know this sound will never be like it used to but so long as I keep improving and tuning this chord, I know it'll get better over time.

One hit of my religion chord and I'm spot on, but just to be on the safe side I'll give the knob a twist or two. This chord will never be pitch perfect all the time, but it's the strongest one I have and without it I wouldn't be an instrument at all.

Now I know my *arte* chord is all good, but if the bow hits it, and I don't like its sound, I'm gonna have to adjust it. EEEK, EEEK–shit way off! I guess no matter how good this chord is, it's just like the others. It's always gonna need its tweets and adjustments.

The last chord is my emotions. There's a lot of us who think we always have this tune in check, but in truth, most of the time this string gets the best of us. So, we must always strive to perfect this sound, no matter how difficult it may be at times. The bow strikes my emotions and I set it back to where it needs to be, however, I'll have to adjust every time it doesn't sound right.

For now, I sound good and have adjusted all these chords to make a sweet melody. I'll have to be tuned up again in the future, but hopefully I've brought out of my case more often until finally I'm out for good and making beautiful music every day. And when that day comes, I pray I'm married with another instrument to produce a symphony led by the greatest conductor of all time.

DANIEL LINO ONOPA

In Tozquitl (The Voice)

Anger, pain, and sadness is what I feel
when I open my eyes and see what is real!
I've been blind for so long, but now that I see,
you will never again succeed in blinding me!
All the injustices you have committed on my people,
you have committed on me, because we are one and the same,
we are equal.
You tell my people to leave but we are here to stay–
aren't you the foreigners anyway?
Yes, yes, I believe the story goes like this:
You are the foreigners who arrived in ships!
How soon you forget the truths of the past–
oh, silly me, I forgot this was an unpopulated land
discovered by ColumbAss!!
Since your arrival, you've spoken nothing but hate.
Is it your jealousy of my people, who you can never emulate?
Every time I turn around another law has been passed
that attacks my people, and it just makes me laugh.
How can you make laws, when you don't respect the ones
already here?!
The ones that say, "Respect all relations and treat Mother Earth
with care."
But how can a people-driven greed respect the earth?
In your eyes it's only dirt that has no worth.
So, take your silly laws and rub them in your filthy chest–
until my people are set free... my spirit will *never* rest!!!

JEREMY OROZCO

Sharing My Appreciation

MY NAME is Jeremy Orozco. I would like to share with you my reason of being thankful for this opportunity to be a part of our cohort program as we strive to learn all we can throughout this experience.

When I first entered the California Department of Corrections (CDC), I was only 19 years old. Today I'm 36, so I've been incarcerated for 17 years. Prior to this prison term, I completed three years in the California Youth Authority (CYA). I was on parole for only a few months. From the age of 13, I've been trapped in the system. I've lost many good years and caused many heartaches for my parents and loved ones all due to my poor choices as a youth with my gang life and drug addiction.

Seventeen years ago, the adult prison system consisted of CDC without the R as today it reads, California Department of Corrections and Rehabilitation. As a young man, with a prison sentence of 28 years, having to do 85 percent of this time, my initial thoughts and goals were to earn a college degree and gain as many job trades as possible. I wanted to make the best out of the situation. This way when the time came for me to return home to my loved ones, I would be a changed man. Everyone would see and know that, yes, I did something positive for myself while I was incarcerated.

However, all of those positive thoughts were quickly diminished when I was faced with a harsh reality. From Delano Prison's Reception Center, I was transferred to Pelican Bay State Prison.

Upon my arrival, the general population yards were in a state of emergency, locked down, due to a serious and fatal riot that happened months prior. My first time in prison, starting off in a full lock-down program with absolutely no rehabilitation opportunities, was a bad situation.

Due to my CYA prior, as well as my young age and gang documentation, I remained on lockdown for a little over three years.

The environment consisted of SHU kick-outs. For the most part many of us were young and gang-related, so things were pretty serious.

As we were released from lockdown, wars were taking place, men were seriously hurt, and I ended up in Administration Segregation (Ad-Seg) a few times.

At the age of 26, I was placed into Ad-Seg and received a validation SHU term as an associate to a certain prison gang. As a result of this, my future consisted of only three options: 1) parole from the SHU; 2) die in the SHU; 3) debrief and be released from the SHU and into any yard. Option 3 was completely out of the equation. Therefore, I was indefinitely stranded in solitary confinement.

The SHU program was nothing new to me due to the many lockdowns and Ad-Seg experiences I already had. The only difference was I knew I wasn't going nowhere until the year 2028, which happens to be my max release date.

A little over eight years is what I spent in the SHU. I made it a point to make every day as productive as possible. I educated myself, worked on self-development, wrote a book for my son, and a few other personal achievements.

My maturity began to progress—my perception of life altered for the better. Furthermore, I started to realize that all of CDC consisted of a big lucrative business—and us prisoners are their living dollar signs. This realization created a fire within me, a fire to learn and build myself into a new me. With the harsh living conditions, and watching some of my peers lose their sanity, I knew I had to do everything I could to survive—I had to return home to my loved ones with my sanity intact.

Then there came a time when a group of well-educated men, of all races and prison groups, joined together and strategized to create the most practical plan for us to fight for our human rights and dignity. This group is known as the Short Corridor Representatives—their utmost objective was to change the gang validation policy, improve the conditions in the SHU, stop CDC from holding human beings in the SHU for 20-plus years, and create more rehabilitation programs throughout the prison system.

Diligently these men led the way; together we fought against the CDC. Class-action suits as well as a petition to the UN was filed. Peaceful hunger strikes were conducted. In 2011, we conducted two hunger strikes. Each one went for the duration of about 19 days with some positive results. In 2013, we conducted another hunger strike that lasted for a total of 60 days. Finally, we started to see major changes to the validation policy as well as the length of time a human being can be held in the SHU, improvement of the living conditions, the implementation of rehabilitation programs, and—best of all—hundreds of human beings released to the general population. Due to the mass release, today Pelican Bay SHU is near vacant.

As for my participation in our peaceful protests, yes, I was involved in each one. The first two hunger strikes I made it through the full length and was rushed to the hospital after they were completed.

With the last protest, my heart was fully committed to make it through the entire way. However, on the 29th day my body succumbed. I was rushed to the hospital and was treated as a trauma patient. An IV was inserted into my chest bone, which was very painful. Days after my admittance to the hospital I went into surgery due to the damage I had inflicted on my body. During my surgery I suffered complications and was given a blood transfusion. Today I live with a permanent health condition as a result of this.

Now, the people who know me, knew I've had a long history of health issues prior to our protests. No one could understand my reasons for participating. I'm sure some individuals may have thought I was a bit crazy.

As I share with everyone, my personal convictions and my own decision to participate are in the nature of this—yes, there was a point in time that I was a stupid kid, with no direction in life, and I made a lot of poor decisions. However, this alone does not justify the fact that CDC did their best to try and destroy me as a human being. My sacrifices were for the betterment of all men who were trapped in the SHU for 20-plus years with no chance of ever being released. Furthermore, for every individual who deserves a chance to participate in rehabilitation programs with the desire to learn and grow into better people, I believe they should be given an equal chance to do so.

With all of this in mind, I think to myself: Just 13 months ago I was sitting in the SHU with no hope. Today, I stand here with you and I'm proud to say I'm a survivor of the SHU. I'm very thankful to be a part of our cohort college program. Out of my 17 years of incarceration, this experience is the first time I've been given an equal opportunity to partake in an educational program. This is an awesome feeling. With a new start, and my hope restored, I believe this experience will play a major role in building me towards a successful future upon my release with my wife and children.

EFRAIN "BEAN" ORTIZ

My Village

Lying at the edge of the water,
on the North East end of Los Angeles,
between the train tracks & the L.A. River,
lies my village, which shines and shimmers.
Its streets lined with tall, palm trees.
Walls occasionally spray painted with graffiti–
those Rascals who were a part of the community.
Let me take you back to Atwater Elementary,
where all the kids sat in class eagerly waiting to cross the street
for a Vince's Ham & Cheese, with no more than fifty pennies.
This was the place I met the following three: David, Jose, and Reeks,
who joined me in pursuit of our destiny–
from Cubs to Bears, and eventually Barristers.
Through it all, no matter what, we stuck together.
Riding bikes through the boulevards to camel back with no regard.
Playing baseball in our sandlot or engaging in street wars
with those Atwater Boys from morning till dawn.
Atwater Village is not just a place called home–
it's the place that created the Fantastic Four.

MIGUEL RENDON

My Life in One Chapter

IT'S SAID to understand someone you need to understand their pain first. I can't help but reminisce about my life and how I came to be where I am today.

From playing marbles in the dirt, to finding ways to avoid taking a bath. I get a kick out of my childhood memories. I have so few I can actually laugh at. I was a kid just like you. Did my best in school, even though it didn't seem good enough. I loved chocolate, like most kids. Although I must admit many times, I stole chocolate from the local Safeway Market.

As you can guess, my poor decision making began early in life. My father was an abusive drunk, a philanderer, who mentally and physically beat his wife and kids! The beatings he gave my brothers and I were more than punishment. They were his way of relieving stress. Taking out it out on whoever angered him that day. Making sure we felt less than—and at times it seemed as if he did it for enjoyment's sake. I wasn't an angel, I admit, but I don't feel I deserved any of those beatings. Nor did my mom or my brother, and, at times, my sisters.

As I grew into my teens, I looked for acceptance from whomever showed me kindness, understanding. A sense of belonging. I looked to whomever, at that time, I believed to be my friends. Unfortunately, they had joined a gang earlier in their lives. So, I joined as well and started carrying a knife for protection. Another poor decision.

I started drinking beer, smoking weed, and since school wasn't important any longer, I began ditching. Now my life was spiraling out of control. I didn't know what I didn't know. Dropping out of school came to me without a second thought. I wasn't much of a gangbanger, nor did the gang mean much to me. The friends I longed for were becoming harder to find. Since we weren't meeting up at school any longer, they no longer thought of me. You'd think my life was crappy enough and couldn't possibly get any worse. You'd be wrong. Not only did I continue to ruin my life, I brought everlasting pain to many innocent human beings. When I took a life and almost another, I went from drinking beer to hard liquor. I was becoming my father.

As I sat with my brother and friends, we drank into the night. On our way to the store for more alcohol, we came across three homeless gentlemen. Our thoughts were to get more money from them. Never did it cross my mind a fight would commence. I would end up stabbing a man to death and nearly another. I took a life with the knife I carried for protection. The pain I caused to their families, friends, and the community is immense and forever.

I was sentenced to life without the possibility of parole at 19 years of age. This brings me to where I am today. For over 30 years I've sat in one prison or another, thinking.

I now understand what my causative factors were, what led to my destructive behavior. Stealing (no matter how small). Allowing my father to physically abuse me and not speaking up to a teacher or other adults. Drinking alcohol at an age, I wasn't mature enough to understand the effects. Joining a gang, carrying a knife, smoking weed, dropping out of school—all these poor decisions led up to the horrible crime I committed. Nothing will undo what I did or bring back the life I took. What I have done to better myself, is to live my life the way my victims would want me to live, in a sense, to honor my victims, to say I'm sorry through how I live. I've earned my GED, earned vocational skills, joined and graduated Victims Awareness, Houses of Healing Group. I now spend my time as a Certified Facilitator (Mentor) teaching others to be empathetic to others and find alternatives to violence. I'm working on a prevention plan for struggling youth. To give kids a safe place to go and someone to speak with. Emphasize the importance of education and the downfalls of gangs. There's no glory in what I did or where I am. Aside from the embarrassment I feel over my past behavior. I brought such shame to my family. Don't be like me. Be a better human being than me.

MANUEL RODRÍGUEZ

A Chirp at the Window

Dedicated to my wife Angie.

I LOOK outside my foggy window. I see and hear a bird chirping. It's a small window in a house of rebar and cement. I never wanted to be no other than myself, but today I wished I was that bird. He is free and could go anywhere. I have to watch and count my steps, can't be out of place, nor out of bounds. He is smart and is always on guard. Two pecks of his food, and he raises his head. Alert, he looks in all directions.

As most of us in the system know, a set of push-ups and our heads look around, not in paranoia but as a mechanism of survival. Has these 11 years of imprisonment made me hate on birds? I know this shit affects all men. I must be trippin'—fuck that bird.

It's the day after, 6 AM, and that bird is chirping again. This time he's got company. Damn that fool be pimpin'! He's got about four female birds on him.

So, I ask myself: What's with that bird? Fuck it, I wish I was a cat so I could tear that bird up. Ja ja.

Oh, shit, it's workout time. As I bump in my cell, stressing on time, doing my routine to help release the stress that easily builds up, I hear that birdy flying and chirping. I ignore the little fucker.

It's been two weeks and I'm not looking out the window. Time. Time. Time. Got to wake up. On time before breakfast. Got to brush my grill at a certain time. Walk the same walk at the same time, Shit at the same time. Yard at the same time. Say buenas noches to my cell at the same time. Time, time, time—why do I trip on time? I'm doing my time, so what's with that? They say insanity is doing the same thing over and over and expecting a different result—like when you circle your routine. Well, today, to switch it up, I will work out at night. I'll show myself I'm not that institutionalized. I guess it's a better way of saying I'm not burned out.

Stupid bird he keeps on pecking at my window. I guess he won. I'm looking at the little dude—he got a blue chest and is building a nest. Good for him. What the fuck? I now hate this bird. He is building his home. While I, a greater creation of God, broke my home. Fuck, who's really the bird again? It's now night time. Without a reason, I'm working out. And, son of a bitch, I find myself working on my wings—ain't that a bitch! As they say, we got to tune in with nature.

So, let's see, the rat that squealed on me fucked up my life. This bird just checked the fuck out of me! I hate I left my cubs and Momma Bear for an enemy prey. Am I trippin' or does this sound like the Discovery Channel? And to top it off, I feel like a jackass.

It just goes to show everything is a learning experience. The past of violence made me a street animal. Genetic trauma comes to play. I found myself and lost the old. That's the gift of me being an imminent transcendent. To change the old. They say birds of a feather fly together.

So, I'm going to stay with positive fly people, with visions of rising. Blue bird, thanks for the lesson. While this cat stays fly and finally learns his lesson.

SAMUEL "BLUFLAME 'EM" SHARAD SHABAZZ, JR.

Apolitical Little Bro'

HOW CAN young brothers ever give the love they were not taught to live and which I'm almost positive most may never know? Many begin to tear apart their relationships right from the start and love never grows because they never cleansed their heart. Still we do not look at ourselves because we envy, hurt, and cuss at each other while making a fuss about the plight we're in... Which shouldn't sound at all strange—most of us refuse to change because each day we still arrange to do these things again. So, yeah, don't sit there looking shocked, for we are those who still block our ears and hearts. We won't unlock them to truly understand while our condition remains the same. When will big brothers ever name themselves as the ones to blame for the problems in our hoods? One of the brothers' greatest fears is letting go our mourning tears that we've collected through the years. And still we do not cry. Yet we cause our women to buy into what we say and things we do. When will it dawn on you that they need to also cry? For crying washes away pride, helps change the way you are inside, so your soul may be the guide it should always be. If you think I'm too sensitive, I'll go ahead and let you live your life, a life that will always create these problems we see. What fight does one think one's fighting when divided into Democrat or Republican? Both parties specialize to demagnetize one's rights. Apolitical little bro, sis, and those likeminded alike...apolitical advocates of equality. So, who needs to vote quadrennial? Because right never changes, it only remains the same. So, no, I'm not dancing at your political party. I'm aware of the adumbrate you speak so I'm going to remain amongst the elite.

Apolitical little bro, sis, and those likeminded apolitical. Represent my walk of life.

THOMAS MICHAEL SIMMONS

Almost...

TEN THOUSAND, one hundred forty-five. How many suns have set over my world to rise upon yours?

Light wanes, specters return, as I float aimless—lost amidst the cold eddies of memory. Each, precious and dear, balanced precariously upon a memory that never fades.

It was almost...

It seems a lifetime ago when a life so graced held a certainty in ability that bore the audacities of possibilities. Now, crushed by the overwhelming weight of profound, relentless grief wrought loss—the loss of you.

Always, I am reminded of you. A sight, a sound, thoughts yield to the soft shuffle of distant feet, to the smell of fresh-brewed coffee you'd place into the microwave a few seconds more to greet another day. I'd close in to steal a frothy kiss as you'd brush your teeth, only to be sprayed as you'd open your mouth and drag the bristles across them. You'd giggle, though, knowing the inevitable was to come.

Whether heartache or heart song, there was ever that gentle smile and caring eyes that bore witness to the wonder you found in everything—and a laugh so clear and pure, no shadow of the heart could withstand.

It was, I was, almost...

A sojourn—ten thousand miles of living along hundreds of paths, then the warm embrace of your arms where, at last, I found solace and home. We'd part, and moments later nothing seemed alright. You were missed.

Now the moments have passed into hours, hours to days, days to years, years to... memory. A memory of that which was...

Almost.

But memory claims a price—the cold reality you aren't here. No words, religious or philosophic, no chaste attempt at explanation could ever help cope with the utter and complete absence of you from my life. It is an unending ache that ages with the scars gazing back from the mirror of a concrete tomb.

Such memory though, the ache makes you more present, now, rather than thoughts destined for an unknown oblivion.

You dwell in my heart, my mind, always—a pole star in this endless night that guides me, yet ever beyond reach.

It was, almost.

Ten thousand, one hundred forty-six. How many suns have set over my world to rise upon yours?

THOMAS MICHAEL SIMMONS

A Yard

Twenty-nine years haunted by regret.
Twenty-nine years of what could have been.
No bitterness, yet shame,
no hatred, despite pain.
To heal and not harm.
My heart and soul screams
to help others' visions come true.
For the impossible exists,
only,
to those who deny the potential of dreams.
As I move onward, to a future uncertain,
to me, a lifetime...
to you, ninety seconds

HANEEF "GENNO" TALIB

Year of Existence

Born innocent, born pure, today I'm none of that.
Robbed of my youth by youths who were robbed of theirs before me.
I've seen a lot early but been through more than I seen.
I leaned on the boys from the park more often than not when kicked out of Jerri's spot.
Forced maturation, maturity before puberty.
Home life and street life kept separate.
Did homework and concealed weapons.
Ticking seconds depict life passing as night replaces day.
Played chicken with the reaper daily.
Tandra told me repeatedly the streets don't play,
Heavy metal to equal the playing field.
Future birthdays stayed in jeopardy.
Avoided the pine box but got trapped in the can.
Doing all I can to get back to her, him, and them.
Hourglass running on "E."
Am I coming or going?
Salat to calm a soul that's hurting.
Taqwa to cool a mind that's been burning.
I'm trying to put layers on an untold evil, but my words hang
        in the balance of conflicting mind,
        unhinged at the temples.
Hard liquor contaminates my temple,
        temporary feel-goodness due to prohibited liquids.
Allah is oft-forgiving.
I'm letting you in... invading my personal,
        conversing with y'all on a personal level.
Today, I'm grateful.
Another year of existence is a milestone.

HERBERT DANIEL TAYLOR

Fate V. Destiny

THE MOMENT I knew I was born to be poor called me into how I would create my own destiny.

I played with my cousins shooting marbles in the dirt. We played in the sandbox that was full of broken glass bottles, crack pipes, and cigarette butts. To us it was a way of life. Riley Tee raised pigeons as if they were his children, clapping his hands to make them tumble from the sky until he clapped them up out of the tumble. Barbecues, basketball games, baseballs, gunshots, dominoes, death, funerals, birthday parties, nicknames, drums, and ice cream trucks. Saturday morning cartoons and music blasting out of each project housing. Low riders, trucks, motorcycles, dirt bikes, weed in the air, loud cursing and fighting. All we knew was that survival was our fate that was dealt to us, and death is our only destiny.

Prison, jail, and death became our destiny, my destiny until I truly found the truth, "Hashem," love, family. All that I went through created who I am today, a righteous figure of change and growth. I have died to be reborn.

HERBERT DANIEL TAYLOR

Red Fog, Black Fog, Gray Fog, White Fog

Red Fog

It is true that anger comes from and is a part of pain. I held onto it not knowing triggers dictated why I lived the way I did. I held on for dear life to my red fog just to feel a part of my mom. My identity was as slow as the fog that moves over the land trembling.

Black Fog

Hold me down, dog. You've been my way of living for a long time, abyss, death, hopelessness. You see black as ugly, but I know you to be real, honest, and forthcoming. You will be what is to come but no understanding.

Gray Fog

How depression has been. The way I lived with no color to identify with. It has been a struggle to allow these mixed emotions and thoughts an opportunity not to always be freed or to know how to be controlled until I took my meds. Hold me down, dog.

White Fog

Why have you forsaken me? I don't want to feel. I don't want to remember. I don't need you now because if I don't feel, it may mean you are beyond my control.

To all you fogs – thank you. Because you remind me that I matter, that I am born to live for me and to die for me. You taught me that when I search, I move like the fog, deliberate, patient, tolerant, and without being stopped. Fog, you remind me you are life and death. You come to existence, then you die. You allow me to see, then you blind me.

DANIEL WHITLOW

Death Jester

Author's note: Trauma is such that it convinces us we lack what we need to make sense of our lives when we want it most. As we lose control, desperation distorts our vision and though we may love life, it becomes unbearable, and the ugliness we see in ourselves (whether real or imagined) fills our eyes with nightmare prophecies. Trauma promotes denial. Denial develops callousness. Callousness kills humanity. Inhumanity kills itself.

Ill-definition in the shapelessness of my companion mental haze
makes absurd hegemonic reliance on form into viscous residue,
clinging to imperiled lacquered layers of quilted uncertainty
—its wet, brown lumpness auguring hopeless equivocations—
resignifying denied attainment as preserved ignorance.
And I accept this and that and more and less than I should.

Every morning's maddening inverted helix descent spiral plummets
as reviled irate seismic demons hide beneath the riled hostile caves
of my sheltered sonic cocoon; my breast-fed illusions of morality
—forge-born perseverance opining tenacious denial of surrender—
negotiate perverted values as garish aesthetics of misused neglect.
How can I remember falling if I never learned to climb?

Ciphered incarnate privations indulge archaic scarcity, like a panicked
mandible bloodstream, onyx tempers twirling with incoherent pulse;
this fucked up pluralized carnage carousel of clown-face corpse entrails
—entailing repulsion's cacophonous rebirth into revolting relevancy—
accentuates the jarring, mealy-mouthed, frayed-nerve-ending atonality
of termite-infested rungs on my rickety developmental ladder.

I will not believe and cannot deny High-Mindedness's lively, lilting prose,
parading a brevity of concern, boasting chasmed consolation bled
of charity,

reaching into the apprehended awestruck darkness jesting compassion to
—rows on rows of teeth and eyes pearl white and wide pleading dry—
broken, shackled bones deteriorating its unmoving cages of
traumatized stone.
(funny thing, scars... with just a slice of a razor, we become something new.)

DANIEL WHITLOW

Cathedral of Doubt

A gesture by the exhausted, bowed head; pausing to absorb a clinging haze,
Like noose-constricted dead at the foot of a breathing mountain
inhale.

A hollow temple revered the empty sockets of nameless skulls,
crushed skeletons of smashed opal altars shrieking distant, flaming curses,
borne on the collapsed backs of penitent heretics scrawling erased words,
fleeing buzzards of prayer; blind, shameless carriers of the soundless Voice
that sears no flesh
and scars no eyes
with lightning burns and shocks of bright—

The absent head rises brooding,
seeking wisdom in unsung songs of bruised and broken servitude;
another stern reminder of fated infatuation—
exhale.

Torn, wasteful flesh beckons with contorted intents from cowardly tombs of lordless filth,
bone fists clutching tattered nothings.
infantile, mindless actions peer through severed veils to solicit witnesses of ruin,
another echoing lament resting ragged on these ancient steps.

Soiled and scarred devoted debts left unpaid—
dust and dirt and blood and shit and darkness decaying in the glorious shadow of an indentured din
obscures the insurgent face,
left to flail wild like a drowning beast, like a servant's heart, to wonder in silence with a mind
possessing a precarious balance upon the liquid face of its joyless dreams.

All languish in this cathedral of doubt—
and while venomous murmurs slither softly down abandoned halls,
and sagging bookshelves bear vast volumes of ash—
only corpses furnish its corrupt space, draped like wet leaves over roots of perdition trees.

Determined to grow from consecrated ground; rebellions' aspect
refusing to rest,
taken the wind, cradled in howling hands.
Sweeping like sifted sorrow through valleys of porous resolve—
to arrange domains of guilt neatly at the feet of an extinct summit—
the sweltering crown of insurrection presses its weary facade against
the stone of gods and sleeps
gasping.

DANIEL WHITLOW

An End with No Beginning

I couldn't be more sincere,
There's nothing I wouldn't do to prove it to you.
We could've laid amongst gravestones,
Sharpened grass growing, from the silently screaming mouths of the buried.

We've lost sight of what we were blind to,
And as undergrowth suffocated, we never figured the end was near.
It was if you poured acid down my throat and restored what was destroyed.

It's the belly of the burdens we shoulder that hungers.
Miserable excuses diminish elusive dreams.
And for all the troubles, we simply walk away?
For now, I struggle to breath, but worry not; tomorrow I'll stop.

I used to imagine what it was like to speak your name,
Ghostly and flat, echoing like a gasping wheeze.
But the night no longer calls to me, it no longer holds the key
to my suffering–it's empty as your silence has left me.

I have dusk in my eyes, as haunting reflections of you manifest before me.
Like torn canvas, the portrait lay in ruin.
Beads of glass where your eyes should be, absently prism colorless energy.
What once was, is no more,

May I still hold you against me?
I couldn't lie to you if I tried, and I've tried.
But I couldn't lie to you if I tried, though I've tried...

ABOUT THE EDITORS

KENNETH E. HARTMAN

Convicted of murder at 19, Kenneth E. Hartman was sentenced to life without the possibility of parole. After serving 38 years, former California Governor Edmund G. Brown, Jr. commuted his sentence and Hartman was paroled in 2017. He's presently a freelance writer who's also working as a development coordinator and prison programs specialist for a Los Angeles-area nonprofit involved in prison rehabilitation programs. His 2009 memoir *Mother California: A Story of Redemption Behind Bars* won the 2010 Eric Hoffer Award. Hartman edited *Too Cruel, Not Unusual Enough*, a collection of prisoner writings about life without the possibility of parole sentences, winner of a 2014 Independent Publisher Book Award. His work has appeared in the New York Times and Harper's.

LUIS J. RODRIGUEZ

Luis J. Rodriguez was a gang member, drug addict, and in and out of jails in Los Angeles during the late 1960s and early 1970s. He turned his life around by the power of the arts, revolutionary study, and social justice organizing. Forty years ago, Luis began work as a journalist/writer during the same time he first entered prisons, juvenile lockups, and jails as poet and teacher. His oldest son, Ramiro, who became gang affiliated in Chicago, ended up serving around 15 years in Illinois state prisons. Ramiro—released now for ten years—often joins his father for talks, circles, and readings including among the incarcerated and formerly incarcerated. Luis is also a multi-genre writer of 16 books, including his latest, *From Our Land to Our Land: Essays, Journeys & Imaginings from a Native Xicanx Writer.*